PACTS & TREATIES

LAND PACTS

SUSAN DUDLEY GOLD

TWENTY-FIRST CENTURY BOOKS
A Division of Henry Holt and Company
New York

To my husband, John Gold, with thanks for his encouragement and support

Twenty-First Century Books
A Division of Henry Holt and Company, Inc.
115 West 18th Street
New York, NY 10011

Henry Holt® and colophon are trademarks of
Henry Holt and Company, Inc.
Publishers since 1866

Published in Canada by Fitzhenry & Whiteside Ltd.
195 Allstate Parkway, Markham, Ontario, L3R 4T8

Library of Congress Cataloging-in-Publication Data
Gold, Susan Dudley.
Land pacts / Susan Dudley Gold.
p. cm. — (Pacts & treaties)
Includes bibliographical references and index.
Summary: Discusses the three treaties that tripled the land holdings of the United
States during the nineteenth century: the Louisiana Purchase in 1803, the
Guadalupe-Hidalgo treaty in 1848, and the Alaska Purchase in 1867.
1. United States—Foreign relations—Treaties—Juvenile literature. 2. Louisiana Pur-
chase—Juvenile literature. 3. Mexico. Treaties, etc. United States, 1848 Feb. 2—Juve-
nile literature. 4. Mexican War, 1846–1848—Territorial questions—Juvenile literature. 5. Alaska—Annexation to the United States—Juvenile literature. [1. United
States—Foreign relations—Treaties. 2. Louisiana Purchase. 3. Mexican War,
1846–1848. 4. Alaska—Annexation to the United States.]
I. Title. I. Series.
E183.7.G657   1997
973.5—dc21   96–44967
                                                     CIP
                                                      AC

Photo Credits
Cover illustration and illustrations on pages 10, 46, 78, and 93 © 1996 North Wind
Picture Archives.
Illustrations on pages 17, 25, 39, 42, and 96 provided by North Wind Picture
Archives.
Illustrations on pages 8, 34, 61, 100, 102, and 105 provided by the Library of
Congress.
Illustration on page 30 from the Collection of The New-York Historical Society.
Maps on pages 6, 15, 21, 36, 49, 52, 56, 70, 73, 76, 81, 83, 85, 90, 107, and 114
© 1997 Susan D. Gold.

Design, Typesetting, and Layout
Custom Communications

ISBN 0-8050-4810-3
First Edition 1997

Printed in the United States of America
All first editions are printed on acid-free paper ∞.
10 9 8 7 6 5 4 3 2 1

CONTENTS

Introduction

Growth Is Destiny

At the beginning of the 1800s, the sixteen states of the United States of America occupied a thin strip of land that ran from the Atlantic Ocean west to the Mississippi River. The new nation occupied less than a million square miles. Most of its 5.3 million people lived in the country. New York City had 60,000 people, and only four other cities had more than 10,000 residents.[1]

By the end of the century, the nation had tripled its holdings. Its population of more than 60 million had set up households in towns that reached from the Atlantic to the Pacific.

Much of the growth was accomplished by three treaties:

- The Louisiana Purchase in 1803.
- The Guadalupe-Hidalgo treaty in 1848.
- The Alaska Purchase in 1867.

The Louisiana Purchase, negotiated with Napoleon's France, doubled the territory of the newly formed United States and accelerated the movement west. It has been called "the most important event of our country since the Declaration of Independence."[2]

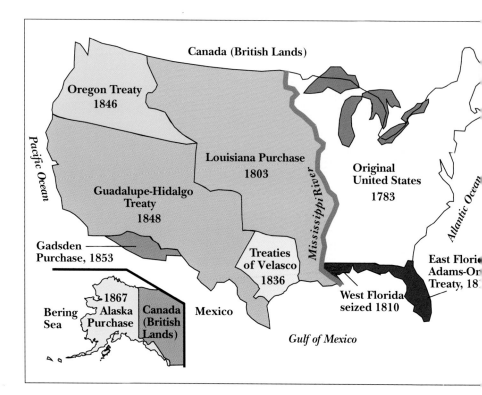

During the 1800s, the United States tripled its land holdings through treaties and pacts negotiated by American diplomats and, in some cases, accepted as the terms of peace.

The purchase of Alaska, ridiculed by some as a worthless, ice-bound land of icebergs and walruses, brought the United States billions of dollars in oil, gold, fisheries, timber, and other resources. Together the two treaties added almost a million and a half square miles of land to the nation's possessions.

Both these treaties were fashioned by diplomats, the first in Paris, France, during Napoleon's reign, the second in post–Civil War Washington, D.C. Once begun, the negotiations progressed rapidly, in the "go-ahead way of the Americans,"[3] as the Russian minister told the czar during the Alaska talks.

What happened after the negotiations ended reflects the changes in technology that occurred in the 1800s. It took two months for news of the Louisiana Purchase signing in Paris to reach Washington, D.C. Sixty-four years later, copies of the Alaska treaty would speed from Washington across the trans-Atlantic telegraph cable to Russia. Within days, Russia's minister in the United States received the Czar of Russia's approval.

Only the Guadalupe-Hidalgo treaty, in which Mexico gave up claims to Texas, California, and New Mexico, came at the cost of American lives. The treaty that ended the bloody Mexican War increased American holdings by a half a million square miles. That and the California gold rush in 1848 brought thousands to seek their fortunes and stake out claims in the fertile valleys of the southwest. It also fueled the bitter fight between slave and free states that would erupt into the Civil War.

The history behind these treaties is the story of America's growth from a fledgling nation to a world power. It is a tale of political plots and great achievements, of flawed men and heroes. The treaties may have been tainted by greed and deceit, but they also bear the mark of idealism and vision. All contributed to America's greatness.

The Louisiana Purchase Treaty

HOW TREATIES ARE RATIFIED

Treaties are agreements made between nations. They may settle boundary disputes, transfer title to property, make peace, resolve disputes, set up alliances, or agree to handle a particular issue in a certain way (for example, banning nuclear tests). The U.S. Constitution gives the president the power to make treaties with the "advice and consent" of the Senate. For a treaty to be valid, two-thirds of the members present in the Senate must approve, or ratify, it. The House of Representatives plays no role in approving treaties.

But often, as in the three treaties in this book, a pay-

8

ment is part of the deal. When that is the case, the House plays a central role in the treaty process. That is because all requests for payment must originate in the House. (If the House approves a payment, the matter then comes before the Senate for consideration. Both the Senate and the House must approve an appropriation for a payment to be made.)

The House does not get to vote on a treaty directly, but it can invalidate a treaty by not approving money required by the treaty.

For example, the Louisiana Purchase was signed by President Thomas Jefferson, and the Senate voted to ratify it by a vote of 26 to 5, more than a two-thirds majority.

The House then had to approve the payment of $15 million for the territory. If the House had voted against the payment, then the terms of the treaty could not have been met and it would have been invalid.

As you read about the three treaties that brought us the Louisiana Territory, much of the southwest, and Alaska, try to follow the political intrigues of those involved. As you do, think for a moment what our country would be like today if just one proponent of acquiring additional land for the United States did not persist and gave up the dream, or if just one vote had gone the other way.

Frontiersmen hunted game in the wild, unsettled lands included in the Louisiana Purchase.

ONE

LOUISIANA PURCHASE

The end of the 18th century marked monumental changes in the world order: the United States had broken away from England to form a new, independent nation; France had overturned the monarchy in a bloody revolution. Now a powerful and charismatic military man, Napoleon Bonaparte, ruled the new France. Europe was in upheaval, as one country after another fell to Napoleon's armies. England, with its still-mighty navy, stood against the French leader, fighting for the survival of its colonial empire.

The United States seemed far-removed from the battles of Europe. Indeed, it took the American ambassador a month to sail from New York to Paris. Sending information to President Thomas Jefferson and waiting for a reply could take up to two months. Yet as far away as Napoleon's France was from the United States, this mighty general—soon to be named Emperor Napoleon—would change the face of America forever. He would accomplish this, not by his sword but by the stroke of his pen.

The story of the Louisiana Purchase and the events leading to its signing is a fascinating tale of intrigue, political maneuvering, and fiery personalities. Let us open with one of the main characters—Napoleon—as he plots to take over the trading routes of the world.

NAPOLEON EYES LOUISIANA

For years, Napoleon, First Consul of France, had been trying to take over the West Indies trade routes controlled by Great Britain. He led his army into Egypt in 1798, with intentions of disrupting the route to India. After heavy losses to England, Napoleon was forced to return home. Now the French ruler was developing a new plan that threatened American trade.

The first step was to regain possession of Louisiana and get West Florida and East Florida from Spain. The Louisiana territory had been under French rule for eight decades, until 1762 when French King Louis XV ceded the land west of the Mississippi River and New Orleans to his cousin, Charles III of Spain, in gratitude for Spain's help during the Seven Years' War.

Napoleon's foreign minister, the sly Charles Maurice de Talleyrand-Périgord, tried to persuade Spain in 1799 to cede the Floridas and the entire Louisiana Territory, "a small part of her immense domains,"[1] to France. By doing this, Talleyrand told King Charles IV, Spain would enlist France's might in protecting the rest of the Spanish lands in the New World. Spain claimed most of South and Central America, as well as much of the land in North America's southwest. Talleyrand said:

> There are no other means of putting an end to the ambition of the Americans than that of shutting them up within the limits which Nature seems to have traced for them; but Spain is not in a condition to do this great work alone. The French Republic . . . will be a wall of brass forever impenetrable to the combined efforts of England and America.[2]

When Spain resisted Talleyrand's proposal, Napoleon sweetened the deal. He offered to create a kingdom for King Charles's daughter and son-in-law, the Prince of Parma. The Prince would become King of Tuscany, a French-controlled territory in Italy with 1 million people. Supported by the Spanish Queen, the deal was sealed in the secret treaty of San Ildefonso, signed by Spain and France on October 1, 1800. The treaty ceded the Louisiana territory to France. Spain retained possession of East and West Florida despite Napoleon's best efforts to win them for France.

THE BATTLE FOR SAINT DOMINGUE

Napoleon's strategy included Saint Domingue (now Haiti), the western part of the West Indies island Hispaniola. The eastern two-thirds of the island was occupied by the Dominican Republic. Saint Domingue was the golden jewel of France's colonies, providing two-thirds of the country's commercial interests. Its lucrative trade centered around coffee, sugar, indigo, and cotton, all farmed by the territory's black population. However, a black general, installed as manager of the colony, was now threatening France's control of Saint Domingue.

In Napoleon's grand scheme, Louisiana and Saint Domingue would be the keys to France's domination of world trade. The tropical land's rich crops would be shipped to New Orleans and throughout the world. With Florida, France would control 400 miles of Atlantic coastline, the Gulf of Mexico, and the Caribbean. It would also regulate the flow of commerce down the Mississippi River and from the surrounding lands.

With the cession of Louisiana to France, Napoleon had only two hurdles to overcome: assure French control of Saint Domingue and somehow persuade Spain to cede the Floridas. He postponed the latter while concentrating on the situation in Saint Domingue.

In 1794, during a struggle with England and Spain for control of the island, France had freed the slaves. Three years later, François Dominique Toussaint L'Ouverture, the son of a slave, had led forces of Haitian blacks against Spanish troops trying to control the island. Known as the "Napoleon of the Antilles," Toussaint had been named general-in-chief of Saint Domingue by the French government as a reward for his triumphant rout and placed in charge of the colony. In a move soon paralleled by Napoleon, Toussaint seized control and was named leader of the island for life, winning the right to name his successor.

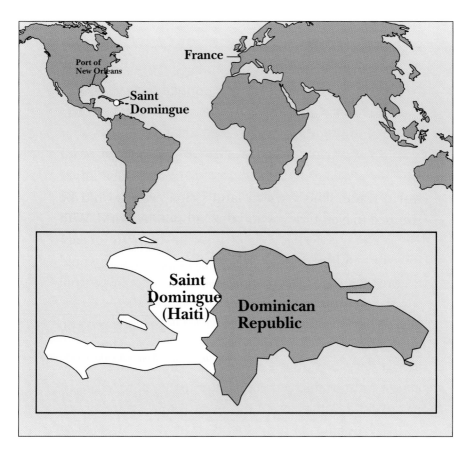

Saint Domingue, pictured above, was to be a stepping stone in Napoleon's plan to control trade in the Gulf of Mexico and Caribbean Sea.

Napoleon, however, still considered Saint Domingue a French colony under his control. He ordered his brother-in-law, General Victor Emmanuel Leclerc, to take over Saint Domingue. Pledging that the colony's blacks would remain free, Napoleon asked Toussaint to assist Leclerc and wrote reassuringly to the black leader: "You know that in all the countries where we have been, we have given it [liberty] to the people who had it not."[3]

Leclerc and an army of 10,000 arrived in Saint Domingue in January 1802, determined to wrest power from the black leader. On February 5, Toussaint's soldiers set fire to the Saint Domingue city of Cap Français, under attack by the French. The flames ignited a war between the races that blazed for almost three months. Poorly armed and with fewer men, Toussaint's forces were no match for the French regulars who had invaded Saint Domingue. By April, the black generals had betrayed Toussaint and surrendered to avoid execution.

Napoleon gave Toussaint his word of honor that he would cooperate with him. Toussaint made the fatal mistake of trusting the ruthless French consul and surrendered to Leclerc. The once-powerful black leader spent his last days imprisoned in a fortress in the Jura Mountains in Switzerland, duped by Napoleon and forsaken by his army.

But Toussaint had his revenge. The fierce fighting of his army had decimated Leclerc's army and the reinforcements that were sent to aid the French effort. Leclerc lost a total of 24,000 men in the bloody battles and to the yellow fever epidemic that followed. An additional 5,000 French sailors lost their lives in the struggle over Saint Domingue.

Napoleon offered the slaves their freedom if Toussaint surrendered. When Toussaint resisted, Napoleon ordered Leclerc to reenslave the blacks on Saint Domingue and to rule them under strict military discipline. When the blacks rebelled, many were massacred with the help

François Dominique Toussaint L'Ouverture fought off the French forces in Haiti but was betrayed by his officers and deceived by Napoleon. He died imprisoned in a fortress in Switzerland.

of Toussaint's former generals, who had allied themselves with the French. On October 7, 1802, Leclerc wrote to Napoleon:

> We must destroy all the negroes in the mountains, men and women, keeping only infants less than twelve years old; we must also destroy half those of the plain, and leave in the colony not a single man of color who has worn an epaulette.[4] [An epaulette is a shoulder ornament worn on a soldier's uniform.]

Saint Domingue would erupt in civil war, Leclerc warned, unless Napoleon sent him an additional 12,000 soldiers to maintain order. The next month Leclerc was dead, a victim of yellow fever. The black generals and troops deserted. Jean Jacques Dessalines, a black general under Toussaint, seized control of the colony. Not only had Napoleon failed to gain control of Saint Domingue; his troops had destroyed its valuable crops and any value it might have had to the French empire.

OPENING NEGOTIATIONS

Meanwhile in Louisiana, the Spanish had not yet transferred power to the French. A new treaty, the Treaty of Tuscany, had been signed by Spain and France on March 21, 1801, officially setting up the Prince of Parma as King of Tuscany. But Manuel de Godoy, Prime Minister of Spain, hated Napoleon and delayed the transfer.

The official ceremony, at New Orleans, that transferred the province from Spain to France would not take place for almost three years.

By June 1801, rumors of the Louisiana cession to France began to make their way to Washington, D.C. Robert Livingston, America's minister in France, asked Talleyrand about the situation. The French foreign minister blatantly denied the existence of such a treaty. Acting under Jefferson's orders, Livingston asked Talleyrand how much France would ask for New Orleans and West Florida. Talleyrand continued to give vague answers. Napoleon wanted to keep the deal secret because he feared the British, with whom he was at war, would attack New Orleans if they knew France owned the territory.[5]

In November, Rufus King, the U.S. minister to England, managed, through diplomatic sources, to get his hands on a copy of the secret treaty. Jefferson, in a letter to Livingston in 1802, expressed his dismay at having the French in New Orleans:

> There is on the globe one single spot, the possessor of which is our natural and habitual enemy. It is New Orleans, through which the produce of three-eighths of our territory must pass to market, and from its fertility, it will ere long yield more than half our whole produce, and contain more than half of our inhabitants. France, placing herself in that door, assumes to us the attitude of defiance. Spain might have retained it quietly for years.[6]

In March 1802, France and Great Britain signed the Peace of Amiens, also called the Treaty of Amiens, ending their hostilities in an uneasy truce. Now Napoleon set out to establish himself on the North American continent. Livingston, still trying to open negotiations with France, published a paper detailing the many reasons why France would be better off selling New Orleans to the United States and distributed it to the French leaders. It seemed to have no effect at all.

On September 1, 1802, he wrote of his frustrations to Secretary of State James Madison:

> There never was a government in which less could be done by negotiation than here—There is no people, no legislature, no councillors—One man is everything. He seldom asks advice and never hears it unasked.[7]

Despite the setbacks, however, Livingston had not completely given up. In the same letter, he told Madison, "I am persuaded that the whole will end in a relinquishment of the country and the transfer of the capital to the United States."[8]

THE CLOSURE OF NEW ORLEANS

It was not Napoleon but a Spanish official's actions that convinced the Americans they had to gain control of New Orleans. On October 16, 1802, Juan Ventura Morales, Spanish administrator at New Orleans, closed

New Orleans was the key trading port for traders and farmers west of the Appalachians.

the port to American traders. Under the terms of the Treaty of Lorenzo in 1795, Americans had been granted the right to deposit their goods in New Orleans free of charge for three years. The right expired in 1798, but the Americans had continued to use the port without objections from the Spanish. Morales decided, on his own, that the Americans should no longer be allowed free use of the port.

The closure provoked such outrage from American traders that war threatened. Some American leaders suspected the French had been behind the closure. Jefferson, however, did not want to risk a war. The fledgling country would have to rebuild its army and replenish its treasury.

Jefferson's goal was to maintain the peace. In a letter to a friend, he wrote: "Peace is our passion, and wrongs might drive us from it. We prefer trying *every* other just principle, right and safety, before we would recur to war."[9]

Pressure mounted as the American traders' goods rotted in warehouses, waiting for the port to reopen. To appease the traders, who threatened to wage war themselves if something wasn't done, Jefferson appointed the popular James Monroe as minister extraordinaire to France. Congress approved Monroe's nomination and allotted $2 million "to defray any expenses which may be incurred in relation to the intercourse between the United States and foreign nations."[10]

Jefferson's instructions to Monroe, who sailed for France in March 1803, offered three alternatives. First, he told the minister to bid high rather than lose the chance to buy New Orleans and West Florida. If the French would not agree to sell, then he was to persuade the French to guarantee American traders the right to deposit their goods at New Orleans. If France refused both offers, Jefferson proposed that the United States offer up to $10 million to buy New Orleans and West Florida. In addition, the French would be granted the right to trade freely in the ports of New Orleans and West Florida for 10 years, the inhabitants of the purchased land would be given the rights of American citizens, and France would be guaranteed possession of the land on the western bank of the Mississippi.

In April 1803, with help from Spain's Prime Minister Godoy, the port of New Orleans was once again opened to American trade. The action appeased the Westerners, but by then Americans knew they had to control the Mississippi.

CHANGING COURSE

Napoleon, who in August had been named consul for life with the right to name his successor, had planned to send an expedition to Louisiana by the end of September 1802. But troops and money had been diverted to Saint Domingue. An armed expedition waiting to sail to Louisiana from Holland had been delayed. By January 1803 it was ice-bound in its Holland port.

In December Napoleon received word of Leclerc's death and the fall of Saint Domingue. He began to re-think his strategy. War had ravaged Saint Domingue's crops of coffee, sugarcane, and indigo; many of the laborers who tended the fields were dead, and Saint Domingue's rich trade was ruined. The blacks were out of control. It would require massive amounts of money and more troops to restore French rule.

Despite the skilled diplomacy of Talleyrand and Napoleon's bullying, France had never convinced Spain to cede the Floridas. The Spanish government, under Godoy's influence, continued to delay the transfer of power in Louisiana.

What had seemed an ingeniously constructed plot had turned out to be a house of cards, built on Saint Domingue as its foundation. Napoleon's bid to use the island colony and New Orleans to control the West Indies trade routes had failed. Louisiana was of no use to him now. It was time to reshuffle the deck.

Napoleon was nothing if not a military man. Trained to respond quickly to crises, he made decisions the same way. Failure was a call to action. A bold new expedition would refocus the world's eye away from the disaster in Saint Domingue.[11]

Where better to direct his forces than England? The Peace of Amiens treaty, signed by France and Great Britain in March 1802, had established a truce between the two countries, but it did not eliminate Napoleon's desire to control the trading routes of the rival nation.

On February 20, 1803, Napoleon harshly criticized Great Britain during his annual report to the French council, known as the Chambers. He turned up the heat even more at a March 12 dinner party. Turning to Lord Whitworth, the British ambassador, Napoleon said, "I find, my Lord, your nation want war again!" An alarmed Whitworth responded, "No, sir, we are very desirous of peace." To which Napoleon replied, "I must either have Malta or war!"[12] Malta, an island in the Mediterranean Sea off the southern tip of Sicily, had been seized by Napoleon in 1798 but was later captured by England. Talk of war soon spread throughout Europe.

France needed to focus all its energies on the upcoming conflict with Great Britain. Napoleon couldn't afford to send armies to protect Louisiana, and he didn't want to risk its falling into English hands. Livingston had been proposing to buy New Orleans for the United States for months. Why not offer him the whole parcel and get it off France's hands?

Napoleon called in Talleyrand. He told him of his plan to sell Louisiana to the United States. Talleyrand had

Napoleon is shown dictating to his secretaries in a painting by Grolleron.

helped Napoleon craft France's colonial empire. Through his skill and persistence, France had finally regained the Louisiana Territory. The Foreign Minister wasn't about to let this cocky young general give it up without a fight.

Talleyrand used all his skill as a master diplomat to persuade Napoleon to reconsider. But once Napoleon made up his mind, he rarely changed course. Angrily, Talleyrand left.

Lucien and Joseph, Napoleon's brothers, were also enraged by the news. Lucien had signed the treaty that had ceded the land to France. Evidence suggests that both Joseph and Talleyrand may have had other motives for not wanting Napoleon to sell Louisiana. Apparently, the British had bribed Joseph with more than 100,000 British pounds to change Napoleon's mind about Malta. When that failed, they offered Talleyrand as much as 2 million British pounds. They reasoned that if Napoleon were occupied in the New World, he would be distracted from his threat to occupy Malta and start another war with England.[13]

The brothers decided to try to convince Napoleon not to relinquish the territory. The morning of March 10, Lucien appeared at Napoleon's door. A servant ushered him into the private chambers where Napoleon was soaking in his bath. The scent of the cologne-perfumed water filled the room. Lucien began talking about the play he had seen the night before. Joseph appeared at the door, and the brothers continued their casual conversation.

Napoleon finally brought up the subject of Louisiana. The brothers told him the Chambers would never allow him to sell the territory. Under the terms of the French

Constitution, Napoleon was forbidden to cede any territory of the French Republic without the consent of Chambers.

Napoleon replied that he had no intention of consulting with Chambers. "The plan which is not fortunate enough to obtain your approbation," he told Joseph coldly, "conceived by me, negotiated by me, will be ratified and executed by me alone; by me, who snap my fingers at your opposition."[14]

Furious, Joseph leaned nearer the bath. His voice, thick with sarcasm, showed his anger: "I tell you, General, that you, I, and all of us, if you do what you threaten, may prepare ourselves soon to go and join the poor innocent devils whom you so legally, humanely, and especially with such justice, have transported to Sinnamary."[15] (Sinnamary refers to a river in French Guiana, where Napoleon banished prisoners.)

Napoleon started to rise from his bath. "You are insolent," he shouted at Joseph. "I ought—."[16] At that point, he threw himself back into the bath. Water drenched Joseph and splashed Lucien. Napoleon's servant fainted, afraid of what might happen next.

But Lucien pretended to be Neptune scolding the waves (from a Roman poem that had been made into a play). The brothers laughed and the tension was broken.

Joseph went home to change his clothes, but Lucien continued his argument with Napoleon. Finally, Napoleon had had enough. He grabbed a nearby snuffbox and smashed it to the floor, threatening to crush Lucien the same way.

Napoleon encountered similar resistance from his

minister of the Navy and Colonies, Denis Decrès, at an Easter Sunday meeting in St. Cloud. Decrès argued vehemently against the sale, but Napoleon's mind was set:

> They ask of me only one town in Louisiana; but I already consider the colony as entirely lost; and it appears to me that in the hands of this growing Power it will be more useful to the policy, and even to the commerce, of France than if I should attempt to keep it.[17]

Minister of the Treasury François Barbé-Marbois—also at the meeting—supported the decision. Barbé-Marbois, who had lived in the United States for several years and married an American woman, was familiar with American ways and friendly with several of the young country's leaders. He understood the American desire for more land and favored the sale of Louisiana.

CLOSING THE DEAL

The next morning, April 11, 1803, Napoleon asked Barbé-Marbois to open negotiations with the Americans. He instructed the minister to ask no less than 50 million francs (almost $10 million) plus an agreement from the United States that it would pay claims its citizens held against France.

(During the Seven Years' War between England and France from 1756–1763, France had seized ships owned by U.S. merchants, prevented U.S. ships from sailing, and looted cargo. The Treaty of Morfontaine in 1800 ended the quasi-war between the United States and France. Still left unsettled was about $5 million in claims by U.S. merchants against the French.)

As they parted, Napoleon told Barbé-Marbois, "I have given to England a maritime rival which will sooner or later humble her pride."[18]

It was not Barbé-Marbois but Talleyrand who approached Robert Livingston later that day with a question. How much would the United States be willing to pay for the entire Louisiana territory? Livingston, who for months had tried to wheedle a response from Talleyrand on selling New Orleans, was flabbergasted. Perhaps 20 million francs, he replied, unsure how to respond to such an amazing proposal. Talleyrand told Livingston the offer was too low and that his suggestion was not an official proposal.

The following day, James Monroe arrived at his Paris hotel. That evening, the Americans gathered at the Livingstons' for a dinner party to greet the minister extraordinaire. While the guests were drinking coffee, Livingston spotted his old friend, Barbé-Marbois, walking in the garden. He invited him in. During the conversation, Barbé-Marbois signaled to Livingston to meet him after the party.

As soon as Monroe left, Livingston hurried to the treasury building, where Barbé-Marbois was waiting. The French minister proposed to sell Louisiana for $20 million (twice the amount Napoleon had asked) plus $5 million set aside for American claims. Livingston protested at such a price. It was 10 times the amount Congress had au-

The slightly deaf Robert Livingston could hardly believe his ears when the French foreign minister Talleyrand offered to sell Louisiana.

thorized Monroe to offer for New Orleans. The United States, he told Barbé-Marbois, had little use for the wild lands of Louisiana. Only New Orleans and West Florida interested the Americans, he said.

Barbé-Marbois agreed that the price was high. He made a counteroffer of 60 million francs (still 10 million more than Napoleon had asked) and the United State's agreement to assume payment of the claims against the French. Livingston, finding it difficult to hide his excitement, said he would have to consult with Monroe, and the two men parted.

It was after midnight when Livingston arrived home. He sat down and wrote a letter to Secretary of State Madison, outlining the offer and claiming credit for himself as the one who had handled the negotiations. "We shall do all we can to cheapen the purchase; but my present sentiment is that we shall buy,"[19] he informed Madison. Well aware of the immensity of the property offered in the deal, Livingston suggested the United States could collect the entire purchase price by selling the unsettled western lands to a friendly foreign country.[20]

On April 14, 1803, Monroe was at last formally presented to Talleyrand as an official representative of the United States. Monroe and Livingston privately agreed to offer as much 50 million francs and the settlement of the American claims in exchange for the Louisiana Territory. In the spirit of negotiation, however, they offered Barbé-Marbois 40 million francs the following day. The French minister took the offer to Napoleon, who, Barbé-Marbois said, "took the offer very coldly."[21] The evening of April 16, Monroe and Livingston upped their offer to 50 million francs. The new offer was presented to Napoleon, and the Americans waited for the French minister's next move.

For 10 days, negotiations for the vast Louisiana lands stalled. Monroe had never quite recovered from his ocean journey and now lay ill in his hotel bed. Napoleon's attention was diverted elsewhere. He announced to Pope Pius VII on April 17 that France was once again at war with England. Hearing the rumblings of war in Europe, the Americans hoped the French would be pressured to sell Louisiana to help finance their army. But they also feared the volatile French leader would change his mind if the deal was not closed soon.

On April 23 Napoleon issued a secret treaty with the Americans, which he presented to Barbé-Marbois. The treaty stated that France would cede the Louisiana Territory to the United States for 100 million francs, that the United States would pay all American claims against the French, and that French trading vessels would have access to six ports along the Mississippi River. Napoleon said he was proposing the treaty as a way to strengthen friendship with the Americans. Since talking with Barbé-Marbois, he had decided to double the asking price. The money would come in handy for his war efforts.

Barbé-Marbois took the treaty to Monroe and Livingston on April 27. At 2 P.M. the three men met at Monroe's hotel, where Monroe, still ill, lay on the sofa. Agreeing that Napoleon's version of the deal was "hard and unreasonable,"[22] the French minister renewed his proposal—that the United States pay 60 million francs plus the American claims.

Meeting two days later, the three men renewed negotiations. Monroe and Livingston again offered 50 million francs, plus the American claims. Barbé-Marbois was firm, however, and the two American ministers agreed to his price of 60 million francs. The total offer was $15 million ($11.25 million—60 million francs—for France and $3.75 million—20 million francs—for the American claims).

At Barbé-Marbois's urging, Napoleon agreed to the terms.

In the Treaty of Ildefonso, Spain had ceded to France "the Colony or Province of Louisiana with the Same Extent that it now has in the hands of Spain, & that it had when France possessed it; and Such as it Should be after the Treaties subsequently entered into between Spain and other States."[23] The exact boundaries of the property were never clearly set forth in the treaty nor in the later pact that transferred ownership to the United States. Later, the Americans were to claim that West Florida was included in the territory, though both Spain and France insisted that it was not.

Livingston pushed for a clause in the pact that would require France to turn over West Florida to the United States if France obtained it. If France did not own the region, then Livingston wanted Napoleon to pledge his help in acquiring it for the United States. Barbé-Marbois refused to include such a clause in the treaty, but he pledged France's help with West Florida.

No one paid much attention to the western boundaries, since much of that land was wild and unsettled except by scattered Indian tribes. The Louisiana Territory was bounded roughly by the Mississippi River on the east,

American negotiators Robert Livingston and James Monroe and French minister François Barbé-Marbois are portrayed in this fresco by artist Constantine Brumidi, illustrating the cession of the Louisiana Territory. The fresco is on display at the U.S. Capitol.

Canada on the north, the Gulf of Mexico on the south, and the Rocky Mountains and the Arkansas and Sabine Rivers on the west. Whether Texas was part of the deal was also a matter of dispute.

Despite the ambiguities, both the French and the Americans were eager to close the deal. The pact was quickly drawn up, first in French, then in English. On May 2, 1803, Barbé-Marbois, Monroe, and Livingston signed the French version of the treaty that gave France 60 million francs in exchange for the Louisiana Territory. The ministers had to wait two or three days while the English version was prepared, which they signed without further delay. After the segment of the pact dealing with the American claims was signed on May 8 or 9, the entire document was predated April 30.

Those signatures doubled the size of the United States. Overnight, the United States grew from a fledgling country of seventeen states to one of the world's largest landowners. (Three states—Vermont, Kentucky, and Tennessee—had joined the original thirteen colonies at the end of the 1700s, and Ohio became a state two months before the Louisiana Purchase was signed.)

The new territory occupied an estimated 875,025 square miles (without the Floridas). It was larger than Great Britain, Germany, France, Spain, Portugal, and Italy combined. In a little more than 100 years, the new region would be carved into 13 states, its vast prairies, mountains, and rivers comprising Arkansas, Missouri, Iowa, Nebraska, South Dakota, almost all of Oklahoma and Kansas, and a large part of North Dakota, Montana, Wyoming, Minnesota, Colorado, and Louisiana.

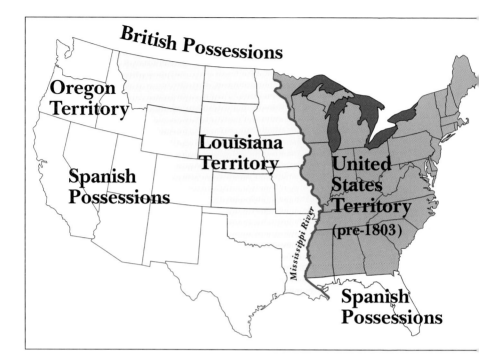

The Louisiana Purchase doubled the land holdings of the United States.

The Louisiana Purchase would eventually pave the way for the United States to stretch across the continent to gold-rich California, Oregon, and Alaska. It would set up the divisions between slave and free states that led to the Civil War. And it would provide the raw resources and growing room that transformed the young nation into a world power.

Livingston, who as a member of the Continental Congress had helped draft the Declaration of Independence and who had administered the oath of office to George

Washington at his first inauguration, understood the importance of the new treaty. "We have lived long," he said to Monroe after signing the pact that granted the Louisiana Territory to the United States, "but this is the noblest work of our lives."[24]

RATIFYING THE PACT

On June 30, news of the treaty reached the United States at last. "Louisiana ceded to the United States!"[25] read the headline in the Boston *Chronicle*'s June 30, 1803, edition. By July 3, the story had made its way to Washington and the rest of the nation. Newspapers of the day referred to the purchase as "the most important event of our country since the Declaration of Independence."[26]

Not everyone greeted the news of the treaty magnanimously. While westerners cheered the purchase, New Englanders feared that the annexation of the new territory would weaken their power. They believed rapid expansion to the west would threaten the union. The young government, they protested, wasn't strong enough yet to hold together a nation so large and widespread.

Though well aware of the treaty's importance, President Thomas Jefferson was nevertheless troubled by the questions raised about the powers of the government. Jefferson had sent Monroe to France with instructions to negotiate for West Florida and New Orleans; Congress had granted the minister $2 million to execute the deal. Both Livingston and Monroe far exceeded their authority when they signed the Louisiana pact.

Now the Senate and the president would be asked to

approve the treaty. The Constitution gave the president the power to make treaties, with the approval of two-thirds of the Senate. Jefferson had long been a strict constructionist, one who believed the federal government and its leaders were strictly limited to those powers listed in the Constitution. His approval of the Louisiana treaty, Jefferson worried, would overstep his authority.

"The Constitution made no provision for our holding foreign territory, still less for incorporating territory into our union," he wrote to John Breckenridge, senator from Kentucky, on August 12, 1803. "The Executive in seizing the fugitive occurrence which so much advances the good of their country, have done an act beyond the Constitution."[27]

To remedy the problem, Jefferson proposed an amendment to the Constitution that would grant the government the right to make the purchase. An amendment, Jefferson noted, would allow the people and the states to have a say in the matter.

But on August 17, Jefferson received a letter from Livingston urging him to hurry the sale through before Napoleon changed his mind. Recognizing the importance of the deal, Jefferson agreed not to submit the amendment, though he said the action threatened to make "blank paper" of the Constitution.[28]

The treaty also stipulated that Louisiana become part of the Union and that its residents become citizens. During debate in the House of Representatives, opponents raised the fear that the huge territory would overshadow the original states. They sought to limit new states to territory owned by the United States at the end of the Revo-

John Quincy Adams, senator from Massachusetts, supported an amendment that would have given the states a say in the Louisiana Purchase.

lutionary War. Others argued that neither the president nor Congress had the right to annex a foreign state.

In the end, though, the deal was too good to refuse. After a day's debate, 90 members of the House voted to support the purchase. Only 25 members, 17 from New England, opposed the measure.

The Senate finally opened debate on the treaty on November 2, 1803. Opponents raised many of the same objections cited by their counterparts in the House. John Quincy Adams, the young senator from Massachusetts who would one day be president, supported the treaty but pushed for an amendment similar to the one Jefferson had discarded. The United States, he argued, "had bought a foreign people without their consent and without consulting the States, and had pledged itself to incorporate this people in the Union."[29]

His motion never got seconded, and the idea was abandoned. The vote on the treaty, when it came, was not surprising. The senators backed the agreement 26 to 5.

TRANSFER OF POWER

When the Spanish heard of the purchase, they were furious. The Marquis of Casa Yrujo, Spain's minister to the United States, accused Jefferson of buying stolen goods.

Spain's biggest complaint, though, was with France. Indeed, France's sale of Louisiana was a blatant violation of the treaty with Spain. First, France had never fulfilled its part of the bargain to set up the Prince of Parma as King of Tuscany. No country other than France and Spain recognized the kingdom. France's troops still ruled there.

Second, France had pledged as part of the treaty never to sell or give away the Louisiana Territory.

In a blistering attack, Chevalier d'Azara, Spanish minister to France, protested:

> This alienation [sale] not only deranges from top to bottom the whole colonial system of Spain, and even of Europe, but is di-

rectly opposed to the compacts and formal stipulations agreed upon between France and Spain, and to the terms of the cession in the treaty of Tuscany; and the King my master brought himself to give up the colony only on condition that it should at no time, under no pretext, and in no manner, be alienated or ceded to any other Power.[30]

Though infuriated over France's treatment, Spain had neither the power nor the inclination to fight the sale. On November 30, 1803, the Spanish governor officially handed Louisiana over to the French.

Before agreeing to the sale of Louisiana, Napoleon had sent Pierre Clément de Laussat to New Orleans to prepare the colony for French rule. Laussat set sail on January 10, 1803, on a mission he anticipated with joy. The arrival of the French prefect in New Orleans on March 26, 1803, was an occasion for celebration among the mostly French population. Brightly colored flags from three nations danced from the masts of 120 ships moored in the harbor. Guns fired a salute to the French official as he rode in a coach to the Government House for a festive reception.

Laussat's proclamation issued to the people of New Orleans upon his arrival was full of rejoicing that the colony had been reunited with France and praise for Napoleon. The separation of New Orleans from France "marks one of the most shameful epochs of her annals," Laussat said. It took Napoleon, "a man to whom nothing

The Old Cabildo of New Orleans, where the Louisiana Territory was officially transferred by France to the United States in 1803

which is natural, great, magnanimous, and just, was new or impossible," to restore the colony to France. "This man, Louisianians, presides over our destinies. From this moment he is the pledge of your happiness."[31]

In a report dated April 5, 1803, and printed in papers in New England the following month, Laussat was said to be "making preparations for the reception of the troops." Foreshadowing what was to come, the article also reported rumors that the troops had been delayed, which had brought "great satisfaction to the friends of the Spanish Government."[32]

In fact, the troops would never arrive, and Laussat's only duties in New Orleans would be to accept the colony from Spain and, 20 days later, relinquish it to the United States.

A spectator named C.C. Robin recorded the scene in New Orleans on December 20, 1803, as Louisiana transferred allegiance once again to become a part of the United States:

Men and women, dressed in their most fashionable clothes, gathered in the square for the ceremonies. As the crowd watched from balconies, galleries, and windows, the French flag was lowered and the American flag raised. A French officer took the flag of his country, carefully wrapped it up, and carried it silently to the rear. While the crowd waited in anxious silence, the American flag was stuck halfway up the pole "for a long time, in spite of the efforts to raise it, as if it were confused at taking the place of that to which it owed its glorious independence,"[33] Robin noted.

Finally, the flag reached the top of the pole. A small

group of Americans shouted "Huzza!"—the Americans' version of "Hooray!"—and waved their hats. The rest of the crowd remained silent, French and Spanish "all moved and confounded their sighs and tears."[34]

"The Louisianian," wrote Laussat, "saw himself with regret rejected for the second time from the bosom of his ancient mother country."[35]

In March 1804, Congress divided Louisiana into two sections along the thirty-second parallel. The southern part became the Territory of Orleans, while the northern part was known as the District of Louisiana (later the Territory of Missouri). In 1812, Louisiana—made up of the lands of the Territory of Orleans—became the nation's 18th state. In May 14, 1812, part of West Florida was annexed to Louisiana after the residents there revolted against Spanish rule.

So Much for So Little

Never before nor since in American history has a peacetime treaty yielded a domain so vast and with such far-reaching effects as the Louisiana Purchase. Years later, recording the dramatic events surrounding the signing of the Louisiana treaty, historian Henry Adams noted the monumental achievement of the Americans in gaining so much through peaceable means.

> In none of these [other treaties] did the
> United States government get so much for
> so little. The annexation of Louisiana was
> an event so portentous as to defy measure-

ment; it gave a new face to politics, and ranked in historical importance next to the Declaration of Independence and the adoption of the Constitution,—events of which it was the logical outcome; but as a matter of diplomacy it was unparalleled, because it cost almost nothing.[36]

The fall of the Alamo inspired Texans to fight for independence and eventual statehood as part of the United States.

Two

SPANISH AND MEXICAN TREATIES

The treaties that led to the annexation of Texas, California, and New Mexico were forged not in diplomatic circles but on the battlefields of the Southwest. In the aftermath, the United States emerged with a half million square miles of additional land that stretched to the Pacific Ocean. The acquisition of the western lands fulfilled the dreams of Americans who had yearned to control the continent. At last, the country "from sea to shining sea" was theirs. But the price had been high: $100 million in war costs and 13,000 American lives.

TRADING FLORIDA FOR TEXAS

American claims to western lands had their roots in the Louisiana Purchase, signed in 1803. In that bargain-basement deal, the French had offered America all the territory west of the Mississippi River that had been ceded to them by Spain. The northwest boundary of the land was never defined, but, according to historian Henry Adams, the western boundary had been set at the Rio Bravo del Norte, also known as the Rio Bravo or the Rio Grande. Included in Napoleon's secret instructions for General Pierre Clément de Laussat, who was sent to supervise the land for France until it was sold to the United States, was a description of the land "bounded on the west by the river called Rio Bravo [Rio Grande del Norte] from its mouth to about the thirtieth degree parallel."[1] This clearly included Texas.

However, Napoleon cagily refrained from mentioning the western boundary to the Americans. When American diplomat Robert Livingston asked for the specific boundaries of the property his country had just bought, French Foreign Minister Talleyrand replied only: "You have made a noble bargain for yourselves and I suppose you will make the most of it."[2]

At the time, Americans were more interested in East and West Florida. West Florida was already developed somewhat, and the southern states saw the area as an extension of their realm. Texas, on the other hand, was a largely undeveloped wilderness, dotted with swamps, deserts, and inhospitable plains.

By the early 1800s, Spain was helpless and dying, a victim of war, revolt, and revolution. In 1810 President James Madison annexed West Florida, claiming that the territory had been included in the Louisiana Purchase. Only Mobile and Pensacola remained under Spanish control in West Florida. During the War of 1812, Americans hoped to gain control of East Florida as well, but

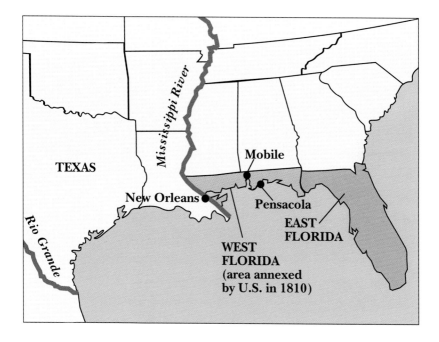

The United States annexed West Florida in 1810, then sought control over East Florida, owned at that time by Spain. The Adams-Onís Treaty gave the United States 37.9 million acres of Spanish lands, including all the Florida territory, at a cost of a little more than 17¢ an acre.

Spain remained neutral. When the treaty with England was negotiated in Ghent, Belgium, in 1814, ending the war, it left East Florida in Spain's hands.

The American quest for East Florida did not end there, however. Spain was occupied with its own problems in Europe and South and Central America, where its colonies were fighting their own revolution for independence. The weakened nation had little real control over the rebellious American settlers in the East Florida wilderness. Without a strong government, the territory became a haven for outlaws and smugglers. Settlers feared attacks from hostile Indians.

Responding to those fears, Andrew Jackson led his army against the Seminole tribe in East Florida. Fearing that the United States would take the area by force, Spain agreed to sell the territory to the United States in the Adams-Onís Treaty, which had been in the works since 1815. The treaty required Spain to give up all of Florida and relinquish rights to land beyond the Rockies north of the 42nd parallel. In return, the United States gave up rights to Texas and agreed to pay American claims (of approximately $5 million) against Spain. The claims had been filed by merchants whose business had suffered during the closure of New Orleans and by shipowners whose ships had been plundered during hostilities in 1799.

Figuring in interest costs, the treaty gave the United States 37.9 million acres (at a little more than 17¢ per acre) and cemented its hold on the North American seaboard. The Adams-Onís Treaty was signed February 22, 1819, by John Quincy Adams, secretary of state under President Monroe, and Luis de Onís, Spanish minister to the United States.

MANIFEST DESTINY

Spain held the rights to Texas for exactly two days. On February 24, Mexican rebels seeking independence declared war against Spain. Mexico took its place among the nations of the world in 1821, modeling its government on U.S. democracy.

At about this time, Americans began to embrace a new philosophy, later called Manifest Destiny. Inspired by the vast lands acquired in the Louisiana Purchase, they believed that the United States was destined to rule North America. A few believed America would someday own half the globe. One way to fulfill that goal, they believed, was to push westward, populating the land with Americans.

John L. O'Sullivan, editor of the *Democratic Review* and the *New York Morning News*, coined the name "Manifest Destiny" in an editorial in which he proclaimed that nothing must stop "the fulfillment of our manifest destiny to overspread the continent allotted by Providence for the free development of our yearly multiplying millions."[3]

Americans migrating west to the lands of the Louisiana Purchase began to work their way along the Red River, into Texas. In 1821, the newly established Mexican legislature gave Stephen Austin a grant to set up American settlements in Texas. Presumably, Mexico believed the Americans would help cultivate the sparsely populated land and make the province more valuable.[4] Austin's grant required him to bring families of sound character, preferably of the Roman Catholic faith (the prevalent religion of Mexico), into Texas. The settlers also had to take oaths of loyalty to Mexico.

For the next dozen years or so, Austin moved his settlers into the region. He tried to live up to his bargain by bringing in decent people who took the oath to Mexico, though most of them were Protestant, not Catholic.

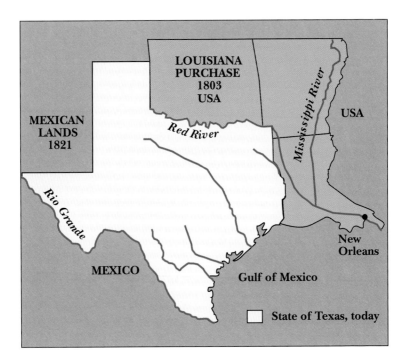

American settlers followed the Red River into Texas, where they established farms and villages on lands sold to them by Stephen Austin and other land dealers.

Other settlers not so willing to pledge loyalty to Mexico slipped into the province under grants issued to land dealers not as scrupulous as Austin.

A British diplomat warned Mexico that allowing Americans to settle on Mexican lands was a bad idea. He said:

> On the most moderate computation, six hundred North American families are already established in Texas; their numbers

are increasing daily, and though they nominally recognize the authority of the Mexican government, a very little time will enable them, to set at defiance any attempt to enforce it. . . . [The settlers are] American—Backwoodsmen, a bold and hardy race, but likely to prove bad subjects, and most inconvenient neighbors.[5]

By the time Mexico realized the danger, it was too late. In 1830, the Mexican legislature passed a law banning new settlers from the United States. But by then, 20,000 Americans had settled in Texas, about twice the number of residents with Hispanic roots. Mexican rule grated on the Americans. They wanted a say in the government of their new homeland. Most of the settlers had come from the American South, lured by the offer of cheap land. Many hoped to build large plantations in the fertile valleys and plains; some had brought slaves with them. Mexico, which did not allow slavery, tried to banish the practice in the Texas province.

By 1832, Austin and his followers were demanding a role in governing Texas. Up until then, they had not paid too much attention to Mexican affairs. Antonio López de Santa Anna, a Mexican general engaged in a power struggle for control of Mexico, promised the Americans he would work to overthrow the central government. Believing Santa Anna would help them gain self-rule, the Americans sided with him.

Once in power, Santa Anna set himself up as a dictator and replaced Texas's legislature with a military governor. It was one of many times the Mexican general managed to gain advantage over his enemies.

At first the Texans tried to work within the Mexican system. In April 1833, Texas leaders held a convention and drew up a constitution to govern themselves. The convention delegates appointed Austin to present their plan to establish Texas as a separate Mexican state to the Mexican legislature.

While many of those at the convention came because they wanted self-rule, others were concerned that the Mexican government might try to reclaim their property. The Austin settlers had grants from the Mexican government, but others had bought land from speculators, traders who bought land with deeds that weren't always valid and sold it quickly at a large profit.

Though the Mexican legislature turned down Texas's request for statehood, Santa Anna granted some of Austin's requests, including lifting the ban on American immigrants and trial by jury. But soon after, Austin was jailed as a traitor, based on a letter he had written urging that Texas set up its own government.

While Austin languished in jail, land speculators and young Texans eager for war led scattered uprisings. In September 1835, Austin was released after almost two years in jail. Frail from his imprisonment, Austin nevertheless spoke strong words. Stating that Texas "must . . . become a part of the United States," Austin declared war against Mexico.[6]

The Texan settlers had originally opposed war, not wanting to risk their farms and crops. But with Austin leading the war cry, they rallied. "TO ARMS!!! TO ARMS!!! Now's the day, and Now's the hour,"[7] proclaimed posters tacked throughout Texas. Volunteers from Texas and the American south, toting muskets and Bowie knives, reported for battle. They carried a white flag with a crude cannon and a single black star on it with the words "Come and Take It" written beneath.[8]

On September 30, 1835, the rough-and-ready band attacked a unit of Mexican cavalrymen. The Mexicans, whose orders had been to confiscate the Americans' cannon but not to wage war, decided to flee. Jubilant, the Texans proclaimed victory. They soon captured the fort at Goliad, a town in the southern tip of Texas along the San Antonio River.

Before too many days had passed, the rebels would arrive at another town along that river and aim their cannon at a mission-turned-fort: the Alamo.

NAPOLEON OF THE WEST

On December 8, 1835, Mexican officers waving a white handkerchief surrendered the Alamo at San Antonio de Béxar to the American rebels. Four days later, Mexican General Mártin Perfecto de Cós led his army of 1,105 men out of Texas. Though the last of the Mexican soldiers had left Texas, the war for independence was far from over. Santa Anna hadn't been heard from yet.

The Mexican president, who called himself the Napoleon of the West, was fully confident that he would

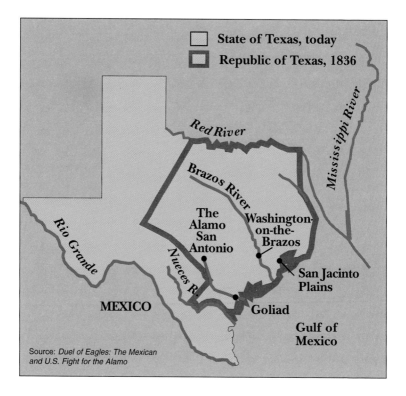

The Texans captured the fort at Goliad, then took over the
Alamo at San Antonio. Later, Texan delegates gathered at
Washington-on-the-Brazos to draw up a constitution.

crush the rebellious Americans like so many ants. He began raising an army of thousands.

After the excitement at the Alamo, many of the American volunteers went home. By the end of January, a mes-
sage from a Kentucky volunteer named Green B. Jame-
son reported that only 114 men remained at the fort, and
only 80 of them were healthy. Under orders from Samuel
Houston, the Texan commander-in-chief, James Bowie
and about 30 volunteers set out to demolish the Alamo.
Houston reasoned that the fort couldn't be defended if it

were attacked by the Mexican army, so it should be abandoned.[9]

But Bowie and Colonel James Neill, who commanded the force at the Alamo, decided the fort served as a key defense against Mexico and should be protected. "Col. Neill & Myself," Bowie wrote to Houston, "have come to the solemn resolution that we will rather die in these ditches than give it up to the enemy. The salvation of Texas depends in great measure in keeping Bejar [the San Antonio area] out of the hands of the enemy."[10] Later, William Travis and his cavalry troop joined the group of resisters, and David Crockett brought volunteers from Tennessee.

On February 23, 1836, Santa Anna and his army arrived in San Antonio. Travis, who had assumed command after Bowie was struck ill, sent off pleas to Texan military leaders to send troops to help defend the Alamo. Santa Anna's men occupied the town and bided their time.

THE ALAMO FALLS

On February 25, the Mexican forces fired on the Alamo to test the strength of the enemy. Gradually, the Mexican army surrounded the adobe mission.

Messengers from the Alamo managed to carry several pleas for reinforcements through the Mexican lines. Responding to Travis's letters, the Gonzales Ranging Company of Mounted Volunteers—under cover of darkness—arrived at the Alamo on March 1. But instead of the expected 700 men from Houston's army, the volunteers numbered only 29, plus three of Travis's messengers.

While Santa Anna's troops and the rebels at the Alamo were preparing for battle, a convention of fifty-nine delegates—including Sam Houston—was meeting in a central Texas town called Washington-on-the-Brazos. On March 2, the delegates signed a declaration of independence and adopted a new constitution, creating a new nation: the Republic of Texas.

During the Convention, while members quibbled over land deals and loans, a messenger brought another urgent plea from the Alamo. "I hope your honorable body will hasten on reinforcements, ammunitions and provisions to our aid so soon as possible,"[11] read the letter from Travis. He had written it immediately after messenger James Bonham had returned to the Alamo with grim news on March 3: no more Texas troops would come to fight against Santa Anna's mighty army. Foreseeing the futility of the battle ahead, Travis also sent a letter to a friend asking him to take care of his family.[12]

On March 5, Travis sent a messenger to tell Santa Anna that his men would surrender in exchange for their lives. The Mexican general denied the request; he would offer no guarantees to the men he considered traitors.[13]

At about 2 in the morning, Sunday, March 6, 1,500 of Santa Anna's soldiers crossed the San Antonio River on wooden bridges and headed for the Alamo. Santa Anna waited with 400 more men to reinforce the advancing soldiers. Just before dawn, a Mexican soldier sounded the bugle, and the Mexican army charged.

The shotguns and cannon of the Texans tore through the approaching Mexican lines, but by daylight, the Mexican army had overrun the Alamo. Frenzied soldiers ran from room to room, searching for rebels still alive and stabbing the dead bodies they found with bayonets.[14]

The soldiers discovered six survivors hiding in a storeroom. General Manuel Fernandez Castrillón guaranteed their safety, offering to take them to Santa Anna himself. The frightened Texans followed the general outside, where blood, gunsmoke, and death permeated everything.

Castrillón pleaded with Santa Anna for the prisoners' lives. As the weary rebels stood there waiting to learn their fate, Santa Anna angrily replied that he would take no prisoners. At his word, the troops shot, clubbed, or speared the defenseless Americans to death. It was 8 A.M., just four hours after the Mexican bugle had summoned the Mexican army to battle.[15]

Santa Anna ordered his men to pile the bodies of the rebels onto pyres and burn them. An estimated 182 rebels died that day; only women, children, and Travis's black slave were spared. The battle had resulted in the deaths or wounding of 600 Mexicans.

A TREATY FOR A LIFE

At Goliad, a fortified city in southern Texas along the San Antonio River, the slaughter was worse. The Mexicans rounded up nearly 500 American prisoners, many of whom were wounded. Under orders from Santa Anna, the Mexican army divided the prisoners into three groups, took them into the prairie, and shot them with cannons and guns at point-blank range.[16]

Spurred on by cries to "Remember the Alamo!" and

by tales of the grotesque slaughter at Goliad, Sam Houston's 700 soldiers were eager to seek their revenge. Eager to win laurels for himself in one final rout of the Americans, Santa Anna led 750 of his men on a quick ride to the plains of San Jacinto, expecting to lure Houston there. Houston got there first.

On April 21, on a sunny afternoon shortly after noon, Houston's rebels hauled their cannon across the plains while the exhausted Mexican army slept. The Mexicans expected the attack to come at night. It took just 18 minutes for the rebels to overpower their unprepared enemy. Trapped between the firing rebels and the lake to their rear, Mexican soldiers tossed down their guns and begged for their lives.[17]

The undisciplined rebels ignored the pleas of their officers to spare the prisoners. Fired by revenge, they shot and clubbed many of the unarmed soldiers to death. Killed in the frenzied mayhem was the Mexican general Castrillón, who had tried to save the Texan survivors at the Alamo.[18]

In a sweep of the area, a rebel search party discovered a Mexican officer hiding in the brush. He wore the plain uniform of a soldier, but his buttons were diamonds. When the party brought their prisoner to camp, the surviving Mexicans hailed him as "El Presidente."[19]

Nearby, Sam Houston lay propped up against a tree, his ankle shattered by a bullet. He invited Santa Anna to sit down. The mighty Napoleon of the West then proceeded to trade Texas for his life. Under the Treaties of Velasco agreed to by Houston and Santa Anna, Mexico would give up claims to Texas, and Santa Anna would or-

Santa Anna surrenders to Sam Houston on the plains of San Jacinto on April 21, 1836.

der the remaining armies—2,500 men on their way to San Jacinto and another 1,000 in San Antonio—to withdraw from the new nation. In return, Santa Anna would be freed.

THE FIGHT FOR STATEHOOD

The Mexican leadership in Mexico City immediately repudiated the Treaties of Velasco, saying they were not valid. They also repudiated the leader who had signed away Texas, and they sent Santa Anna into exile. But with its government in upheaval, a huge debt, and the army in disarray, Mexico put off further action against what it still considered to be a renegade province.

The Texans almost immediately asked to join the United States. President Andrew Jackson rejoiced at the news from San Jacinto but nevertheless postponed his answer. Presidential elections were coming up, and Jackson didn't want to hurt the chances of his hand-picked candidate, Martin Van Buren. Jackson knew Northern states would object to Texas's annexation because they didn't want to see more slave states join the union. The night before he left office, however, Jackson nominated a consul to represent the United States in Texas. The Senate confirmed the appointment the next day.

Van Buren, a Democrat like Jackson, continued to delay the annexation of Texas, believing it would make the growing division over slavery even worse. Most of the Whigs also opposed the annexation and western expansion, which they saw as a way for Southerners to spread slavery. In fact, Representative John Quincy Adams, a leading Whig of the day and former president, held the view that Texas's fight for independence had been a plot by Southern slaveholders who planned to migrate to Texas with their slaves and extend Southern power.[20]

A joint resolution in the House to annex Texas, proposed in the summer of 1838, never came up for a vote. Adams blocked debate by filibustering, talking continuously, from June 16 until the House adjourned on July 7.

For the next five years, Texans tried to join the Union and failed. The chances of Texan statehood became more remote when the Whig Party's candidate, William Henry Harrison, beat Van Buren for the presidency in

1840. When President Harrison died after only a month in office, John Tyler took over the post. The Whigs had put Tyler, a Virginia Democrat, on the ticket to attract Southern voters. Though he opposed Jackson, Tyler supported states' rights and was suspected to be sympathetic to the South's views on slavery.

Rejected by the Whigs and spurned by the Jacksonian Democrats, Tyler became a president without a party. He was mockingly called "His Accidency" by his enemies. During this time, Northern abolitionists stepped up their attempts to ban slavery in the United States. The abolitionists presented petitions to Congress almost every day to abolish slavery in the District of Columbia, to stop the slave trade between states, and to guarantee that slavery would not extend into areas outside the South. They stood against the Texas annexation because they opposed the creation of another state that allowed slavery.

Sam Houston, now president of Texas, was becoming frustrated over the United States's reluctance to annex his country. "If Texas goes begging again for admission to the United States, she will only degrade herself,"[21] he told his supporters. Houston began to hint that Texas might seek support from France or England, both of which had recognized the Republic as an independent nation.

Tyler, alarmed at Houston's implications that Texas might join with England, began to work harder to bring the Republic into the Union. In the fall of 1843, Tyler sent Secretary of State Abel P. Upshur to discuss a treaty of annexation with Texas. When Upshur was killed in an accident, the new Secretary of State John C. Calhoun continued negotiations.

Meanwhile, those who favored Texas annexation had not given up the fight. Some Northerners as well as Southerners favored expansion as the nation's "manifest destiny." Robert Walker, a senator from Mississippi and an ardent supporter of expansion, was one of the leaders in the fight.

Tyler knew he would have to drum up support in the Senate for any treaty proposing annexation. The president sought out his friend Walker's help. Walker was a man "supremely self-confident" in his abilities to win people over to his viewpoint.[22] He decided to aim his campaign at the moderates in both parties.

In January 1844, Walker wrote "A Letter to Northerners." The 32-page document used moral, economic, and political arguments to support his case for the annexation of Texas. It was supplemented by pages of statistics. Among his points were the following:

- The United States cannot afford to let Texas be taken over by England. That would open up the Gulf coast to attack by both British and Indian enemies.
- Texas is a lucrative market for the North's industries, trade, lumber, and mining interests. As part of the United States, its people will buy tariff-free supplies and services from the North.
- Instead of extending slavery, Texas will help end slavery in the United States.

Expanding on the last point, Walker argued that the

large plantations in the South were depleting the soil. Eventually, the plantations would have to move elsewhere to support the large slave population that ran them. The logical choice of a new site was Texas. Once all the slaves moved into Texas, Walker said, the Southern states would join with the Northern in supporting the Union and rejecting slavery.[23]

Walker further argued that eventually the Texan soil would also be depleted. The plantation owners would have no other place to go. They would have to choose between keeping their slaves and going bankrupt or freeing them. Walker contended that the logical choice would be to free the slaves, who would then migrate south to Mexico and South America. In this way, the Texas annexation would rid the United States of slavery.[24]

If Texas did not join the Union, Walker argued, the Republic would soon be controlled by England or Mexico, both of which banned slavery. Texas would no longer serve as a "safety valve" for the slavery problem. Once the Southern plantation owners could no longer afford to maintain a large slave population, slaves would be freed to the North. There, they would compete with white workers for jobs, live in poverty, and hike crime rates. Walker argued that the white North would never accept blacks into their culture; whereas, Mexico and South America already had a large population of mixed races and people of color.[25]

Walker's letter, first published in the *Washington Globe* on February 3, 1844, was read by millions. It was later reproduced as a pamphlet and in newspapers throughout the nation.

Many leaders in the fight against slavery were outraged at Walker's biased views against the black race. They charged that he had distorted figures to support his unproven claims. Some even implied that Walker was being paid off by Texas land speculators and that he was a speculator himself.

In June 1844, Secretary of State Calhoun presented the annexation treaty to the Senate for approval. A strong antislavery faction in the Senate blocked its passage.

The Senate adjourned, and politicians prepared for the upcoming presidential campaign. Discarding Tyler, the Whigs nominated former Kentucky senator Henry Clay as their candidate. Martin Van Buren had been the leading contender for the Democratic nomination, but he opposed the annexation of Texas. The Democrats decided to go with James Polk, a supporter of expansion who favored Texas statehood.

Walker and his supporters heated up the campaign with their own brand of rhetoric. Walker prepared a second pamphlet, this time addressed to Southerners, titled "The South in Danger," which stated that Southerners should support the Democrats as the party that favored the annexation of Texas. He labeled Clay a candidate of the Northern abolitionists and accused him of wanting to destroy slavery.[26]

Clay and others opposed the annexation of Texas because they feared it would not only cause a serious split between North and South but also lead to a war with Mexico. The Whig leader called the annexation "dangerous to the tranquillity of the country, unjust to Mexico, and dishonorable in the eyes of the world."[27] But Clay, sensing that voters were shifting their views in support of annexation, muted his opposition at the end of the campaign. An abolitionist, James G. Birney, drew enough votes from Clay to give the election to Polk. He won with 49.6 percent of the votes cast.

In the end, Walker's arguments may have convinced enough antislavery Northerners to support annexation to tip the election. Twenty-three years later, he would play a similar role in the fight to win approval for the annexation of Alaska.

Tyler took Polk's election as a sign that the public supported the Texas annexation. He sent a joint resolution to Congress to annex Texas. On January 25, 1845, the House approved the annexation. Walker then personally delivered the resolution to the Senate. Three days before Tyler was to leave office, the Senate approved the annexation of Texas by a vote of 27 to 25. Unlike a treaty, which two-thirds of the Senate must approve, a joint resolution can pass with a simple majority. In one of his last acts in office, Tyler signed the resolution into law.

Texas, after waiting so long, voted almost unanimously to accept the annexation. On December 29, 1845, the Republic of Texas joined the Union as the twenty-eighth state.

War with Mexico

Polk knew a war with Mexico was inevitable. Mexico had always suspected that the United States had plotted the Texas war in order to take over its northern land. The annexation and statehood of Texas confirmed that belief.

Charging that the United States had committed an "act of robbery,"[28] Mexico broke off relations soon after Texas's annexation. In Mexico's view, the United States had stolen one of its provinces.

Polk dealt with the situation in two ways. First, he sent John Slidell to Mexico with an offer of up to $30 million for its northern territory, upper California and New Mexico. When Mexican leaders refused to see Slidell, Polk ordered General Zachary Taylor to take his army to southern Texas. Mexico demanded that the Americans leave the area, which Mexico claimed was not part of Texas. Taylor's army then blockaded the Rio Grande. In response, Mexican troops fired on the Americans on April 24, 1846.

This was the shot Polk had been waiting to hear. Since he hadn't been able to buy Mexico's northern lands, the president decided war was the only way to claim California and New Mexico. But he didn't want to be the one to start the war.[29] Polk heard the news of the incident on May 10. He immediately called together his cabinet, then told Congress that Mexico "has passed the boundary of the U.S., has invaded our territory and shed American blood upon the American soil . . . war exists, and notwithstanding all our efforts to avoid it, exists by the act of Mexico."[30]

Three days later, on May 13, 1846, Congress declared war on Mexico.

The action was not without its critics. Representative Thomas Corwin of Ohio protested: "If I were a Mexican, I would tell you, 'Have you not room enough in your country to bury your dead men? If you come into mine we will greet you with bloody hands and welcome you to hospitable graves.'"[31]

Writer Henry David Thoreau was so opposed to the "immoral" war that he went to jail rather than pay his poll tax to support it. After the war had ended, Representative Abraham Lincoln criticized Polk's efforts to blame Mexico for starting the war as "the sheerest deception" and questioned whether the shots were fired on U.S. soil.[32]

Polk expected the war to be brief. Mexican leaders, too, believed that the war would be over soon, but they thought Mexico would be the victor. The nation's army, dressed in flashy, red uniforms, appeared to be stronger than it was. Mexico, only 25 years old, had endured years of unrest as one dictator after another claimed power, then was removed. The country was deeply in debt with barely enough money to pay for supplies for the army.

The American war effort focused on taking over California and New Mexico and securing the Texas border. Polk ordered Colonel Stephen W. Kearny to move along the trail to Sante Fé and into California.

While Kearny was making his way to New Mexico, a brash explorer named John Frémont was busy in California. Even before war was declared, Frémont and an armed band of adventurers—Kit Carson among them—had entered California and challenged the general of the Mexican province. They left before fighting erupted and made their way to Sacramento. There a small group of rebels had proclaimed independence for the Republic of California and on June 16, 1846, raised a white cotton flag made from Annie Frisbie's white petticoat and decorated with a big star and a grizzly bear.

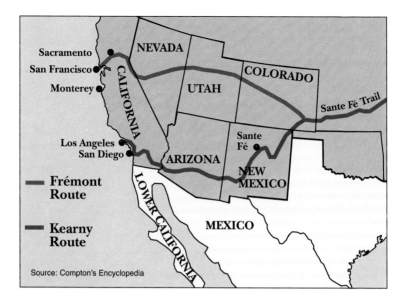

Americans under Colonel Stephen W. Kearny and John Frémont took over New Mexico and California.

(A day later, on June 15, 1846, England signed a treaty that gave the United States a large parcel of land that would later become the states of Oregon, Idaho, and Washington.)

Frémont put himself in charge of the band of Sacramento rebels and began his "conquest" of California. When the group arrived in Monterey, they learned that the United States was at war with Mexico. Commodore John Sloat, who had been sent to patrol the Pacific Coast, had taken over the Custom House in Monterey on July 7, 1846. On July 9, the Stars and Stripes replaced the Bear Flag at Sacramento. A few days later, Sloat's forces occupied San Francisco. In mid-August, Commodore Robert Stockton, who replaced Sloan, helped Frémont capture Los Angeles without much trouble. Stockton officially annexed all of California on August 17, 1846.

Meanwhile, Kearny had marched his motley army of Missouri militiamen, Mormons, and regular soldiers into Sante Fe. The Mexican governor, who had no desire to fight, agreed to retreat, and in August Kearny claimed New Mexico as an American territory. He then headed for California.

By this time, the residents of southern California—a mix of Mexicans and Mexican-Americans who considered themselves Californians—had rebelled against the harsh rule of the U.S. military leaders. In September, an army of about 200 rebels seized control of southern California. However, the combined forces of Kearny, Stockman, and Frémont recaptured the territory by mid-January 1847. After only eight months, the United States controlled what had been Mexico's northern provinces.

AMERICAN VICTORY

Polk was eager to end the war quickly once he heard that California and New Mexico had been annexed. He ordered General Taylor to lead his army into Monterrey, Mexico. The Americans claimed victory there on September 23, 1846, after a fierce, three-day battle.

The army then marched to Buena Vista and waited for the Mexican army, led by Santa Anna. The resilient general had regained power in 1839 and been deposed once again. From his exile in Cuba, he had watched as his homeland tangled with Americans. This was his chance, and he took it. Suavely, he offered to negotiate a peace with Mexico. The Americans believed him and slipped the wily general through their blockade of Mexico harbor. As soon as his feet touched Mexican soil, he proclaimed himself as Mexico's savior. Then he rounded up an army of 20,000, which he immediately led to defend his nation from the Americans.[33]

Bunkered down at Buena Vista, the Americans finally saw the Mexican army approaching. Though the Mexicans had marched through the desert in winter, with little food and water, they were still a sight to see. Santa Anna led them, clad in a uniform of brilliant red and black, trimmed in gold. The self-proclaimed Napoleon, confident that he could overpower the smaller American army, sent a letter to Taylor warning him to surrender or his army would be "cut to pieces."[34]

Taylor refused. On February 22, 1847, Santa Anna led his men in hand-to-hand combat. During the siege, Taylor, astride his old white horse, shouted encouragement to his men. "Give them a little more of the grape[shot], Captain,"[35] he told an officer. The slogan would carry Taylor into the presidency two years later.

Unable to dislodge the Americans from their stronghold after a two-day attack, the Mexican general ordered his men to retreat. At the battle's end, more than 700 U.S. soldiers had been killed or wounded, but twice as many Mexicans died. Though Santa Anna tried to claim victory, the Battle of Buena Vista crushed his army's spirit.

Instead of ordering Taylor to continue the push to Mexico City, Polk shifted that duty to General Winfield Scott. Polk, a Democrat, feared that if the popular Taylor won the war, the Whig general would be elected president. Scott, also a Whig, was a less likely hero with his pompous ways.[36]

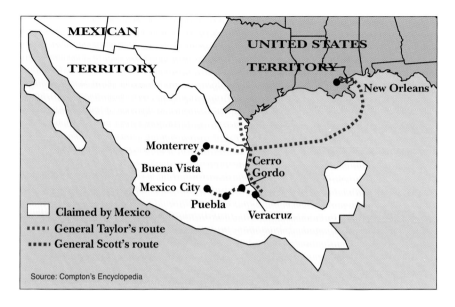

MEXICAN
TERRITORY

UNITED STATES
TERRITORY

New Orleans

Monterrey
Buena Vista
Mexico City
Puebla

Cerro
Gordo

Veracruz

☐ Claimed by Mexico
▪▪▪▪▪ General Taylor's route
▪▪▪▪▪ General Scott's route

Source: Compton's Encyclopedia

After forcing the Mexican army to retreat at Buena Vista, the American forces seized Vera Cruz, then marched to Mexico City, the Mexican capital.

General Scott sailed from New Orleans, landing on Lobos Island seven miles south of Vera Cruz on March 9, 1847. Packed into specially built surfboats, the troops made it ashore without interference from the Mexican army. After surrounding the city and cutting off the water supply, Scott seized Vera Cruz. The Mexicans surrendered the city on March 28, 1847.

The next stop was Mexico City, the Mexican capital where Santa Anna had marched with his army. Following a path scouted by Captain Robert E. Lee, who would one day lead the Confederate army, Scott led 10,000 soldiers toward the capital. Along the way, they defeated Mexican soldiers trying to block off the Cerro Gordo pass. The

Americans reached Puebla, about 75 miles from Mexico City, on May 15, 1847.

Many of the men in Scott's army were volunteers, who had signed up for twelve months' duty. Now their time was up. Ignoring Scott's pleas to stay, they left for home, reducing the size of the army by one-third.[37]

Scott decided to station his army in Puebla for the summer, while he waited for new recruits. Finally, in early August, Franklin Pierce and his soldiers joined Scott's troops. Together, the two armies scaled mountain passes 10,000 feet high. At last, they saw Mexico City, nestled in the valley below. Awaiting them were Santa Anna and 25,000 Mexican soldiers, protected by stone causeways that crossed the marsh surrounding the city.

During the night, the American forces overran the northern flank of Santa Anna's army. Three miles from Mexico City, Scott suggested a ceasefire while the two leaders negotiated a treaty. Santa Anna agreed but instead used the time to reposition his troops. Two weeks later he led his army in another attack.

Waiting until nightfall, Scott led his troops on a direct assault of the city. Climbing up ladders under fire from the Mexican defenders, the American soldiers scrambled up the high walls and bayoneted their attackers. After a bitter battle, Santa Anna's army surrendered on September 17, 1847. One-third of the Mexican army had either deserted or was killed in the fierce campaign to protect the capital. The Americans lost 900 soldiers in the battle.

Foreseeing an American victory, Polk had sent Nicholas P. Trist, chief clerk of the state department, along with Scott's army with instructions to offer Mexico up to $25 million for its northern lands. Now, with Scott's brilliant success, the president wanted better terms. Some Americans were even calling for the annexation of all of Mexico.

In November, Polk ordered Trist to return to Washington to discuss his new instructions. Following Scott's advice, the clerk ignored Polk's orders. He stayed in Mexico and worked to finish the negotiations for the peace treaty as quickly as possible. Both men feared the unstable Mexican government would collapse before the terms were approved. Santa Anna had once again been sent into exile.

On February 2, 1848, Trist and representatives of the Mexican government signed the treaty at Guadalupe-Hidalgo, a small town about three miles from Mexico City. The town got its name from Father Miguel Hidalgo, an early leader in Mexico's fight for independence from Spain.

Mexico agreed to cede California and the Territory of New Mexico (which included what is now the states of New Mexico, Arizona, Utah, Nevada, and parts of Oklahoma, Kansas, Colorado, and Wyoming) to the United States and accepted the Rio Grande as the southern boundary of Texas. The United States agreed to give Mexico $15 million and pay off $3.25 million in claims U.S. citizens had filed against the Mexican government.

Polk was furious at Trist for ignoring his orders. He accused the clerk of being an "impudent and unqualified scoundrel"[38] and later had him arrested. But the negotiations had been concluded, and the president signed the treaty. On March 10, 1848, the Senate ratified the treaty

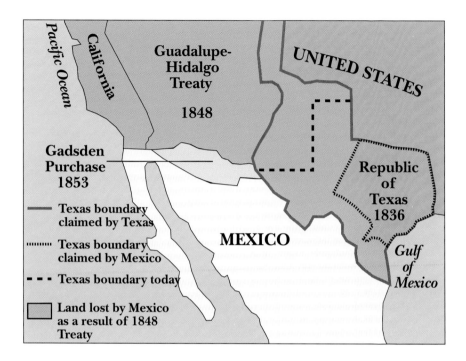

As a result of the American victory in the Mexican-American War, Mexico lost its claims to California and the Territory of New Mexico as well as Texas. The Gadsden Purchase, signed in 1853, transferred another 30,000 square miles of land from Mexico to the United States.

by a 38 to 14 vote. Whigs who had opposed the war supported the deal because they feared it would be replaced by one that gave the United States possession of all of Mexico.

DESTINY OR UNHOLY LAND GRAB?

For believers in Manifest Destiny, the victory over

Mexico confirmed the righteousness of their dream. In Mexican terms, the war and the treaty were an unholy land grab. But Americans believed they were doing Mexican citizens a favor. They thought their country's "democratic institutions were of such magnificent perfection," writes historian Ray Allen Billington, "that no boundaries could contain them. Surely, a benevolent Creator did not intend such blessings for the few; expansion was a divinely ordered means of extending enlightenment to despot-ridden masscs in nearby countries!"[39]

Soon the lure of gold would bring thousands to the new western lands of the United States. Adventurers and then settlers would go there by ship, by wagon train, and later by rail.

Construction of a rail system that spanned the nation resulted in another purchase of land. To build the transcontinental railroad, the United States had to gain a right-of-way south of the Gila River on land owned by Mexico. In December 1853, James Gadsden, American minister in Mexico City, negotiated a deal with Mexico for almost 30,000 square miles. The Gadsden Purchase, for which Mexico received $10 million, expanded the United States' southern territory to what is now southern Arizona and the southwestern tip of New Mexico.

Under the Compromise of 1850, engineered by an elderly Henry Clay, California entered the Union as a free state. New Mexico and Utah became territories free to decide for themselves whether to allow or ban slavery.

The compromise only postponed the inevitable Civil War to come. But the Union would survive, and tales of glory would continue to feed the western dream.

The vast lands of Alaska and its key role in trade with the Far East made it valuable in the eyes of U.S. expansionists.

THREE

ALASKA PURCHASE

A t the head of the powerful Mississippi River in St. Paul, Minnesota, William Seward surveyed the vast lands of a country that he hoped one day would stretch far beyond what he could see. That day on the banks of the Mississippi—September 18, 1860—he told of a dream he himself would help fulfill:

> Standing here and looking far off into the northwest, I see the Russian as he busily occupies himself in establishing seaports and towns and fortifications, on the verge of this continent, as the outposts of St. Petersburg, and I can say, "Go on, and build up your outposts all along the coast up even to the Arctic ocean—they will yet become the outposts of my own country—monuments of the civilization of the United States in the northwest."[1]

Within the decade, Seward would sign a treaty ceding to the United States a territory twice the size of France. For 2¢ an acre, the land mockingly called "Seward's Folly" became an American possession. It would one day join the nation as the forty-ninth state, Alaska.

TRADE AND THE GREAT COUNTRY

In the fall of 1860, William Seward, an ambitious lawyer and skillful politician, was on the campaign trail for his party's nominee, Abraham Lincoln. Seward had barely missed winning the nomination himself.

Born in New York, Seward served as a state senator and as governor for two terms. As a U.S. senator from New York, he played a leading role in the battle against slavery. Early in his political career, Seward had embraced the philosophy of Manifest Destiny. He believed that it was the destiny of the United States to occupy all of the Americas. But unlike Napoleon and other expansion-minded Europeans, Seward did not pursue war as a way to accomplish this goal. Instead, Seward believed that people to the north, south, and northwest would see the benefits of living in a democracy and would eventually ask to join the Union of their own free will.

Trade and wealth were the keys to the nation's successful expansion, Seward believed. Trade would help the country's economy grow, and the traders would carry word of America's freedom and success into other lands. In the Senate, Seward backed the development of the transcontinental railroad, supported international trade agreements, and pushed for commercial growth within

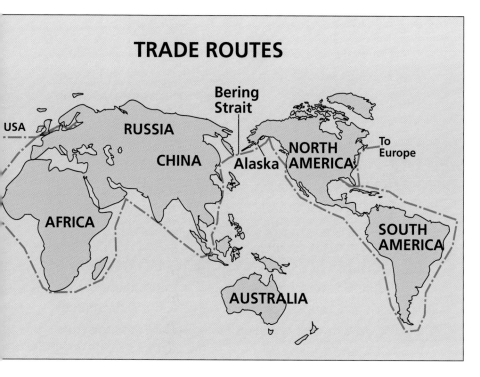

TRADE ROUTES

Bering
Strait

USA

RUSSIA

CHINA

Alaska

NORTH
AMERICA

To
Europe

AFRICA

SOUTH
AMERICA

AUSTRALIA

*American ships sailed around South America to Alaska to ob-
tain furs to trade in China.*

the country. He once told a friend: "Our population is
destined to roll its resistless waves to the ice barriers of the
North, and to encounter Oriental civilization on the
shores of the Pacific."[2]

America's interest in trade with the Oriental countries
of the East began with the trade mission of the New York
vessel, *Empress of China,* in 1784. The first American ship
to trade in China, it was followed three years later by
Boston's *Columbia* that sailed around South America to
the Northwest Territory on the Pacific Ocean. There the
ship bought furs from the Indians and traded them for
tea in China.

The fur trade boomed when merchants discovered that the Chinese would pay large sums for the pelts. One of the best places to hunt for furs was Russia America, in the far northwestern corner of the North American continent. The land would one day become known as Alaska, the English version of *Al-ay-ek-sa*, which in the Aleutian language means "the great country."

RUSSIAN-AMERICA COMPANY

Alaska had been under the control of Russia since the 1700s. At the request of Russian Czar Peter the Great, Vitus Bering, a Danish captain serving in the Russian navy, set sail off the coast of Russia in search of North America. His first trip ended in failure, but on October 9, 1741, Bering spotted St. Elias and other mountains rising in the mist along Alaskan's southern coast. Landing on what is now Kayak Island, he is credited as being the first European to set foot on Alaskan soil. After exploring the island, Bering and his men landed on several other islands off the mainland, then discovered and named several of islands in the Aleutian chain.

The old adventurer was eager to return home with news of his discoveries. But death, not glory, awaited him. On November 5, high seas forced his ship to land on an island off the eastern coast of Siberia. There, storm-driven waves wrecked the ship. The men sought shelter on the island through the long winter. On December 8, huddled in a hut and sick from scurvy, Bering died. The island was later named Bering Island in his honor.

In their struggle to survive, the Russian crew members

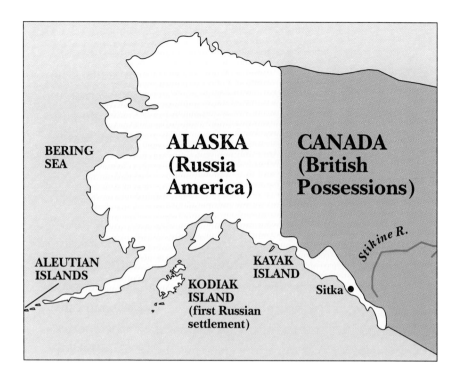

Danish sea captain Vitus Bering, an officer in the Russian navy, landed on Kayak Island in 1741 and claimed Alaska for Russia.

hunted sea otters and seals, eating their flesh and using the warm pelts for protection against the cold. By August 1742, they had managed to rebuild the ship and finally landed on the Russian mainland. Long given up for dead, the explorers caused quite a stir in their homeland. Their tales of Alaska and the beautiful pelts they brought back from their journey inspired others to follow the new route to North America.

Adventurers and fur traders soon headed for Alaska to make their fortunes. The gentle Aleutians were enslaved and forced to hunt for the valuable furs. By the late

1700s, only half of the original native population remained.[3]

In 1784, Grigory Ivanovich Shelikov established the first permanent Russian colony in America on Kodiak Island. Four years later, the Empress of Russia granted Shelikov's fur trading company exclusive rights to the surrounding area.

Shelikov appointed Aleksandr Baranov as agent in charge of his fur-trading operation in the territory east of Kodiak Island. Under Baranov's leadership, Shelikov's company and a second fur trading firm in another part of Alaska joined to become the Russian-American Company. Its territory included all of Alaska. A contract with the Russian government granted the company "full privileges, for a period of twenty years, on the coast of Northwestern America, . . . the exclusive right to all enterprises, whether hunting, trading, or building, and to new discoveries."[4]

Baranov took full advantage of his position as manager of the fur monopoly and, later, as governor. He lived in an elegant home, lavishly furnished with European fixtures, polished wood floors, an extensive library, and even a private art gallery. Traders gathered at Baranov's table late into the night, feasting on the best foods and drinking large amounts of alcohol. Anyone not wishing to party with the wild-living Baranov was eliminated from the list of those allowed to trade with his company.[5]

By the early 1800s, the Russian-American Company was firmly in control of the Alaskan territory. Traders from America and England's Hudson's Bay Company did business with the natives when they could, but in 1821

The Russians, Americans, and English battled over access to Alaska's rich fur trade.

Russia issued a proclamation banning foreign traders from Alaska. Treaties between Russia and the United States in 1824 and with Britain in 1825 allowed traders from those two countries to trade on a limited basis in Alaskan waters.

The treaties didn't smooth Alaskan relations between Russia and other nations for long. In 1834, Russian warships prevented a Hudson's Bay Company expedition from sailing up the Stikine River, where it planned to establish an outpost. The following year, the Russians banned U.S. traders from Alaskan ports. In 1841, Russia renewed its contract with the Russian-American Company, giving it control over the colony for the next 20 years.

Western Americans continued to hunt for whales and fur-bearing animals in the waters off Alaska's coast. The territory's fur trade and Alaska's role in trade between North America and the East soon caught the attention of Senator William Seward and his friend, Senator William Gwin from California. Both strong proponents of expansion, the men saw Alaska's potential as a stepping stone to the lucrative markets in the Orient. In 1852 they won federal funds to explore and map the area "for naval and commercial purposes."[6]

By the fall of 1853, Russia and Turkey were embroiled in the Crimean War. As Great Britain prepared to enter the fray against Russia, the Russian merchants who ruled Alaska became uneasy. With its powerful navy, Great Britain would have no trouble overpowering Alaska if England decided to take over the region's trade route. Peter Kostromitinov, the Russian vice consul at San Francisco and an agent for the Russian-American Company, came up with a plan to trick England. He proposed that his company transfer all its "property and franchises" to the American Russian Commercial Company, a San Francisco firm, for three years.[7]

The contract, signed by the two firms on January 30, 1854, was sent to the Russian representative to the United States, Edouard de Stoeckl, for his approval. Stoeckl conferred with Gwin and Secretary of State William Marcy. All agreed that the contract would never fool England into thinking Alaska was no longer a Russian territory.

Worried that the contract would draw the United States into the Crimean War, the Americans advised Stoeckl to veto the plan.

Several newspapers carried reports of the deal after someone leaked the details of the contract. According to the *New York Herald*, Russia wanted to cede Alaska to the United States. Other papers picked up the story and expanded on it. A July 25, 1854, editorial in the *Herald* reported that Russia had already offered the territory to the United States.[8]

Instead of going through with the plan to deceive England, the Russian-American Company forged a deal with the English-owned Hudson's Bay Company. Under the pact, both companies agreed to respect each other's property in North America. Hudson's Bay Company controlled the vast territory surrounding Hudson Bay. That included Ontario; Manitoba; and parts of Quebec, Saskatchewan, Alberta, and the Northwest Territory. With the deal in place, England agreed not to attack Alaska. Later, a Russian diplomat speculated that England agreed to the Alaskan deal because it feared the United States would take over the territory if it was threatened by England. Others suggested Alaska was not worth the trouble to England.[9]

The flurry of publicity piqued the interest of American expansionists. Gwin and Marcy asked Stoeckl if the papers might be right: Did Russia want to sell Alaska after all? Stoeckl said no, and the meeting ended. But Stoeckl now knew that the United States might be interested should Russia ever want to sell its North American territory.

The Treaty of Paris ended the Crimean War in 1856. Russia, left with huge national debts, looked for ways to rebuild the treasury. Grand Duke Constantine, brother to Czar Alexander II who now ruled Russia, suggested that the country consider selling Alaska. On April 3, 1857, Constantine told the czar: "We should do well to take advantage of the excess of money at the present time in the treasury of the United States of America and sell them our North American colonies."[10]

Constantine warned that if Russia didn't sell Alaska, the United States would sooner or later take control of the territory on its own. Other Russians wanted to keep Alaska. Baron Ferdinand Wrangell, chairman of the board of the Russian-American Company, argued that Russia would be giving up an important source of income from the Alaskan trading posts. He estimated the worth of the territory at $5.6 million, but said the value of the area could more than double in the future. Prince Alexander Gorchakov, Russia's foreign minister, favored delaying any negotiations until the Russian-American Company's contract expired in 1861.

Constantine, determined not to let the matter drop, ordered a study of the Russian-American Company to determine its value to Russia. He also told Stoeckl to "carefully advance" the notion of buying Alaska to the American leaders in Washington.[11]

Meanwhile, businessmen in the United States were looking toward Alaska as a route to the lucrative trade with the East. In a letter to Secretary of State Marcy in

1857, businessman Perry McDonough Collins estimated the market for U.S. cotton fabrics in Russia and North China would bring up to $1 million a year.[12]

In December 1859, Gwin repeated the question he had asked Stoeckl five years before: Would Russia be willing to sell Alaska? The sale, Gwin reasoned, would give American merchants a trade route to the East and would ease tensions between American fur traders and the Russians.

Stoeckl must have been delighted to have Gwin approach him about a sale that Russia was already considering. He asked Gwin to submit a formal proposal. Gwin reported back that President James Buchanan was interested in buying Alaska, but he couldn't risk making a public offer. Admitting the territory to the Union would upset the balance between free and slave states, and prospects of the sale would heat up the debate already raging between North and South.

Stoeckl sent word to Russia of American interest in Alaska, along with his recommendation to sell the territory. The $5 million Gwin had mentioned sounded like a good price to him. Gorchakov, however, still wasn't sure the sale would be in Russia's best interest. He told Stoeckl to push for a higher price and to stall the sale until the expiration of the Russian-American Company contract.

Gorchakov's stalling tactics turned out to be unnecessary. By the time Stoeckl received Gorchakov's orders in April 1860, the sectional dispute over slavery had boiled over. If Buchanan were to propose the sale, Congress would automatically reject it, Gwin reported. The senator advised Stoeckl to wait until the following year when a

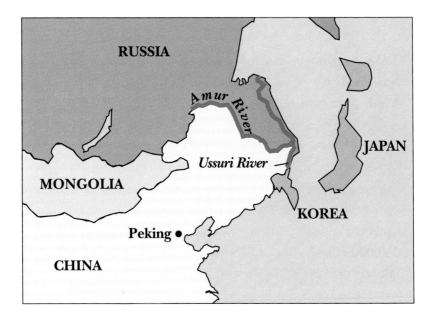

The Treaty of Peking gave Russia control over the trade route that ran along the Ussuri River to Korea.

new president would be in power. But by the time Abraham Lincoln took his oath of office, the nation was heading for war. It would be almost seven years before Russia and the United States would resume the Alaska talks.

FRIENDLY RELATIONS

In Russia, the case for selling Alaska was building. The Treaty of Peking, signed in November 1860, granted Russia control over the land on the eastern bank of the Ussuri River and south to Korea. The country also gained the right to travel to Peking. With these advantages, Russia no longer needed Alaska as a trading outpost.

By early 1861, Grand Duke Constantine had received the results of the Russian-American Company study. It revealed that the monopoly on trade held by the Russian-American Company had stunted economic growth in Alaska, led to widespread smuggling, and discouraged Russians from settling there. The report recommended that the Russian-American Company's monopoly not be renewed. If the company insisted on a monopoly, then the report proposed that the Russian government take over control of Alaska. Such a move would be expensive, however. Some estimated it would cost Russia at least 250,000 rubles (about $188,000) a year to administer the faraway colony.[13]

In the United States, the Civil War exploded with the first shots fired at Fort Sumter on April 12, 1861. Lincoln ordered a blockade of Southern ports to cut off supplies. This move threatened France and England's thriving textile mills, which depended on American cotton. France, hoping to end the blockade, offered to mediate the dispute between North and South. The Union refused, not wanting to give concessions to the South.

Russia, no friend of England or France, refused to support the call for mediation. The Union was grateful for Russia's support. Seward, who had accepted Lincoln's request to serve as his Secretary of State, sent a thank-you to Stoeckl. Russia, he said, "has our friendship, in every case, in preference to any other European power, simply because she always wishes us well, and leaves us to conduct our affairs as we think best."[14]

In 1863, Russians faced a war of their own. Polish nationalists seeking independence from Russia rebelled, and France and England threatened to intervene. Not wanting its fleet to be trapped in port by a blockade of the more powerful English navy, Russia sent several warships to America's northern ports.

The Northerners, still in the midst of the Civil War, thought the Russian fleet had come to support their cause. Crowds cheered the Russian officers and crews, and great banquets and parties were held in their honor. President Lincoln held a reception at the White House for the crew of the *Alexander Nevsky*. Though some of the American leaders guessed the real reason behind the Russian visit, the American people never learned the truth. The episode cemented relations between the two nations and paved the way for the friendly negotiation that would lead to the Alaska Purchase.

ESCAPE FROM DEATH

On April 9, 1865, the Confederates' General Robert E. Lee surrendered to the Union's General Ulysses S. Grant at Appomattox. The Civil War was over.

Five days later, the Russians almost lost their most important ally in the Alaska negotiations. On April 14, 1865, John Wilkes Booth shot Lincoln to death as he watched a play at Ford's Theatre. Booth's associate, Lewis Powell, alias Lewis Payne, sought to kill Seward as well. As Lincoln's secretary of state and right-hand man, Seward was seen as a powerful force behind the president's policies.

Several days before Lincoln's assassination, Seward had badly injured himself when he jumped from his out-of-control carriage as it careened behind runaway horses. The night Booth killed Lincoln, Payne made his way to the Sewards' house, where the sixty-three-year-old secre-

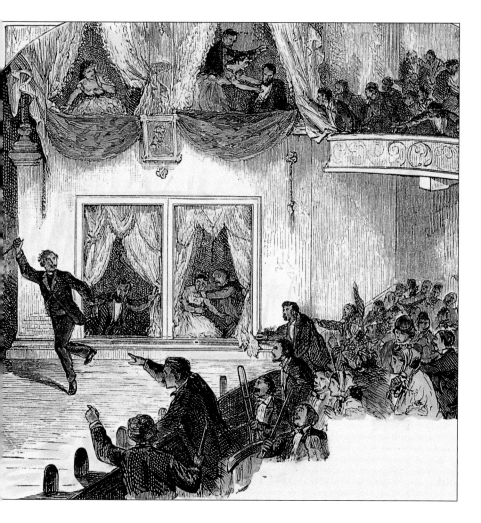

On April 14, 1865, John Wilkes Booth assassinated President
Abraham Lincoln. At the same time, Lewis Payne, an associate
of Booth, tried to assassinate William Seward.

tary lay in bed. Pretending to deliver medicine to Seward, Payne managed to get inside the house. Suspicious, Seward's older son, Frederick, tried to stop Payne. The would-be murderer knocked the young man unconscious with the butt of his gun. Payne jumped Seward's male nurse and slashed him with a bowie knife. He then attacked the delirious Seward, stabbing him in the throat and face. Rescuers found Seward on the floor, unconscious and suffering from deep wounds. He survived the ordeal but never completely recovered from the attack. A long scar on Seward's neck where Payne had tried to slit his throat was a clear reminder of his escape from death.[15]

After Lincoln's assassination, Andrew Johnson—a Southerner with no real base of power—became president. He asked Seward to continue as secretary of state, and Seward agreed. From that post, he continued his efforts to expand the United States.

In the years following the Civil War, many Americans abandoned the Manifest Destiny philosophy that had driven families to settle Texas and California. They focused, instead, on rebuilding the towns destroyed by the bloody battles of war and reorganizing the government that had so recently been divided in two.

Seward, though, along with a few other leaders, had never given up on the vision of an ever-expanding America. But after the Civil War, he discarded his view that all the country needed to do was wait and people would come knocking on the door to join the Union. He believed now that the government should speed up the expansion by buying land. Alaska presented the perfect opportunity to put his theories into practice.

The Russians had never renewed the Russian-American Company's contract in Alaska after the company refused to operate without a monopoly. That left the Russian government with three choices. Russia could:

- Go on as before, with Alaska under the exclusive control of the Russian-American Company. In that case, trade and conditions in Alaska would no doubt continue to decline.
- Run the colony itself, but it would cost a great deal to set up a government, run schools, and provide services for the inhabitants of Alaska. It would also be difficult to administer Alaska from faraway St. Petersburg, the capital of Russia.
- Sell Alaska to the United States.

The last option began to look like the best. As the Christmas holidays of 1866 approached, five Russian leaders hurried to a meeting called by Czar Alexander to discuss the Alaska dilemma. Gathering in the palace in the center of St. Petersburg were Alexander, Constantine, Gorchakov, Stoeckl, Finance Minister Mikhail Reutern, and Minister of the Navy Nicholas Krabbe. Constantine and Stoeckl had already urged the czar to sell Alaska to the Americans. This time even Gorchakov did not hesitate. Supporting the plan, he noted that Alaska's sale to the United States would weaken England's hold on Cana-

William Seward believed Alaska was an important key in developing trade between the United States and the Orient.

da. In addition, the sale would strengthen the friendship between Russia and America.

Alexander agreed. He gave Stoeckl the go-ahead to begin negotiations. But, he cautioned, it must look as if the idea originated with the Americans. The Czar didn't want the world to think mighty Russia was so weak that it was auctioning off its properties.

In Alaska, things went on as before. Even without a contract in effect, the Russian-American Company continued to control Alaska. In 1866, Seward heard from two groups complaining about Alaska's closed ports. The Washington territory's legislature, at the request of businessman Joseph Lane McDonald, had asked President Andrew Johnson "to obtain such rights and privileges of the government of Russia, as will enable our fishing vessels to visit the harbors of its possessions."[16] McDonald's firm, the Puget Sound Steam Navigation Company, had hoped to obtain a lease to fish in Alaskan waters but had been denied. Fur dealer Louis Goldstone had also sought a lease and been refused. Sporadic disputes between Russians and American whalers and fur traders also added to the bad feelings threatening to mar the friendship between the two countries.

As Seward considered what to do about Alaska, Stoeckl set sail for America. The stage was set for negotiations to begin in earnest.

TREATY SIGNED

The two men who were to take leading roles in the Alaska deal were both accomplished politicians. American Secretary of State William Seward had worked to improve education and defended the rights of Irish Americans during his stint as a New York state legislator. Known as "the Governor" to those who remembered him in that role in New York State, he had prominent ears and "a slouching, slender figure." Historian Henry Adams described him as having "a head like a wise macaw; a beaked nose; shaggy eyebrows; unorderly hair and clothes; hoarse voice; offhand manner; free talk, and perpetual cigar."[17] At the time the negotiations began, Seward was almost 66 years old.

Russian minister Edouard de Stoeckl had served as part of the Russian delegation in Washington for many years. Appointed charge d'affaires in 1854, he became Russia's minister to the United States in 1857, a post he held for almost a dozen years. Fluent in English, charming and sophisticated, Stoeckl had dark, curly hair, a bushy mustache and sideburns, and deep-set, intense eyes. He had married an American woman and enjoyed the social life in Washington. People called him "the Baron," though he had no real title.

Stoeckl arrived in New York on February 15, 1867. He stayed there for three weeks while he recovered from a sprained ankle suffered during the rough trip across the Atlantic.

The weekend of March 9 to 10, Stoeckl traveled to Washington, D.C. On the following Monday, he visited Seward at the State Department. Seward used the visit to discuss the complaints brought to him by the frustrated traders and fishermen blocked from Alaskan ports. Stoeckl told the secretary of state that Russia would never issue a commercial lease to a foreigner. Seward asked about opening Alaskan waters to U.S. fishermen. No, Stoeckl replied, Russia would not agree to that either.

Stymied, Seward then asked if Russia might consider selling Alaska to the United States. That was the opening Stoeckl had been looking for. Yes, he said, Russia would consider an American bid for the territory. Surprised, Seward said he would have to consult the president and the cabinet and get back to Stoeckl.

On Thursday, Seward met again with the Russian minister. President Johnson had given his approval of the plan, Seward reported. The United States, he said, would pay $5 million for Alaska. When Stoeckl did not respond, Seward upped the price to $5.5 million. Stoeckl suggested they discuss the price after Seward had had a chance to talk with the cabinet.

By the next day, Seward had prepared a draft treaty to show the cabinet. Meeting with them and President Johnson, Seward asked for $7 million to buy Alaska and the Aleutian islands. The request surprised them, but they unanimously approved the purchase.

Seward and Stoeckl resumed negotiations the following week. The cabinet, Seward said, had authorized him to spend no more than $6.5 million on the deal. Encouraged by Seward's willingness to raise the price, Stoeckl demanded $7 million. Seward was in a rush to get the treaty to the Senate before it adjourned in a week. Under the U.S. Constitution, treaties must have the approval of the president and two-thirds of the Senate. The secretary reluctantly agreed to Stoeckl's price providing he throw in the property of the Russian-American Company (owned

Edouard de Stoeckl,
Russian minister to the
United States

by the government but certainly not worth $500,000). On March 23, 1867, Stoeckl and Seward agreed to the terms. The deal was set.

Stoeckl cabled the details of the treaty to Russia. On March 29, he received approval from Alexander with two minor requests. Under the terms of the treaty, the United States would take possession of Alaska as soon as the signed treaties had been received in both countries. According to the original terms worked out by Stoeckl and Seward, payment for the territory would not be made for ten months. The czar wanted the payment sooner, and he wanted the money to be paid in London. But he gave Stoeckl the power to negotiate the treaty as he saw fit.

After receiving the telegram, Stoeckl went to Seward's house to tell him of the czar's response. "Tomorrow, if you like," Stoeckl told Seward, "I will come to the department, and we can enter upon the treaty."[18]

Knowing that the Senate was scheduled to adjourn the next day, Seward replied: "Why wait until tomorrow, Mr. Stoeckl? Let us make the treaty tonight."[19]

Stoeckl, used to a more leisurely pace, protested that it was evening and no one would be at the State Department to process the treaty. Seward had a ready answer: "If you can muster your legation together before midnight, you will find me awaiting you at the department, which will be open and ready for business."[20]

Before heading for the office, Seward asked his son Frederick to summon Senator Charles Sumner, chairman of the Senate Foreign Relations Committee. The senator went to the Seward house, where Frederick and Stoeckl explained the treaty to him and asked for his help in obtaining approval from the Senate. Sumner, who had heard nothing until that moment about the negotiations, made no promises. As Sumner left for home, Stoeckl asked him, "You will not fail us?"[21] But the senator did not answer.

Stoeckl hurried to the State Department. He told Seward of the czar's requests, but Seward resisted making the changes. He had reasons for denying them. First, he knew the request for $7 million to pay for Alaska would have to come before Congress, and the House wouldn't meet again until December. Second, he wanted to take immediate control of Alaska. Ever the shrewd politician, Seward knew members of Congress would find it difficult to lower the U.S. flag and return the territory to Russia once Americans had claimed it as their own, which the

William Seward, U.S. Secretary of State, seated at left, and Russian Minister Edouard de Stoeckl, with hand on globe, signed the Alaskan Purchase treaty on March 30, 1867.

United States would be required to do if Congress refused to appropriate money to pay for Alaska.[22]

Stoeckl agreed not to push his demands, but in return he added another $200,000 to the pricetag. Seward agreed. At 4 A.M. on March 30, the two men signed the treaty ceding Alaska to the United States.

Seward was in the Senate chambers before 10 that same morning. The secretary of state chatted with several of his friends in the Senate, telling them of the treaty and seeking their support. The Senate was scheduled to adjourn at noon for a long recess. Seward wanted to make sure the senators approved the treaty before they left on their break.

That morning President Johnson formally submitted the treaty. Senator Sumner made a motion to refer the matter to his Foreign Relations Committee. The senators approved the motion and agreed to hold a special, private session on the treaty the following Monday.

The treaty came at a bad time for the Johnson administration. The Radical Republicans in Congress bitterly opposed Johnson's policies of leniency toward the Southern states. The Radicals, who controlled Congress, frequently voted down Johnson's projects and overrode his veto.

With this in mind, Seward began an all-out publicity blitz to win support for the Alaska treaty. Thurlow Weed, publisher of the *Commercial Advertiser* in New York and Seward's old friend, printed a detailed report of the treaty in his paper's second edition March 30. "Grand Acquisition of Territory" and "Our Pacific Coast Line Doubled" read the headlines.[23]

Another friend of Seward, editor Henry J. Raymond, pushed for the treaty in the *New York Times*. Opponents, however, had their own friend in the press, Horace Greeley, publisher of the *New York Tribune*. Greeley, who had gained fame for his advice to young men to "Go West," was a longtime foe of Seward. He charged that Seward and Johnson were using the treaty as a way to divert attention from their political problems. Greeley dubbed Alaska "Walrussia" for its walrus population and claimed the land was worthless. Others referred to the northern territory as "Seward's Folly" and "Seward's Icebox."

Seward, however, persuaded war heroes, businessmen, and others to support the treaty. Many wrote letters to the *New York Times* praising the deal. Professor Spencer Baird of the Smithsonian Institute released a lengthy statement detailing the benefits of Alaska. "The shores of the North Pacific," he said, "are swarming with animals of economical importance, cod, salmon, fur seals, etc."[24]

After meeting in a closed session on April 1, the Senate adjourned to listen to voters' opinions on the matter. Seward used the time to good advantage. Beginning March 30 and for the next 10 days, he hosted dinner parties for key members of Congress. Over wine and gourmet food, he treated his guests to a relentless recital of Alaska's glories. During this time, Seward also released a thick packet of material outlining the benefits of the territory.

Seward got some unexpected help from leading Radical leaders. Representative Thaddeus Stevens from Pennsylvania had opposed Johnson at almost every turn and had tried to remove Seward from office. But he favored expansion and spoke in support of the treaty.

Sumner, who had been reluctant at first to back the plan, became its most ardent supporter. He said if the Senate opposed the treaty, westerners would see it as the

PREPARING FOR THE HEATED TERM.

King Andy and his man Billy lay in a great stock of Russian ice in order to cool down the Congressional majority.

Opponents of the Alaska Purchase nicknamed the territory "Seward's Icebox" and "Seward's Folly."

work of antagonistic easterners. But he resented Seward's handling of the affair. The secretary of state should have included the Senate in the negotiations, Sumner believed.

Nevertheless, under Sumner's guidance, the committee voted to approve the treaty on April 8. Only two senators opposed the measure, William Pitt Fessenden of Maine and James Patterson of New Hampshire. Fessenden, who referred to Alaska as "Seward's Farm," said he would vote to approve the treaty only "with an extra condition that the secretary of state be compelled to live there and the Russian governor be required to keep him there."[25]

Sumner presented the treaty to the full Senate at 1 P.M. that afternoon. Once again meeting in closed session, the senators listened while Sumner argued for passage. In a detailed, three-hour speech, Sumner described Alaska's geography, resources, and history. Then he outlined the points in favor of the treaty: its position as a trading outpost linking U.S. goods to Oriental markets, the opportunity it presented to repay Russian kindness during the Civil War, and its role in expanding U.S. territory.

"The present treaty," said Sumner, "is a visible step on the occupation of the whole North American continent. By it we dismiss one more monarch from this continent."[26] During his speech, Sumner suggested the territory—up until then referred to as Russia America—be called Alaska.

Swayed by Sumner's support, the Senate approved the treaty on April 9, 1867, by a 73 to 2 vote. Fessenden once again voted in the negative, as did Justin Morrill of Vermont.

Following the vote, Stoeckl sent the treaty to Russia for Alexander to sign. The first battle had been won.

HOUSE INTRIGUE

Most Russians thought their country had got the best of the bargain. The *Narodnii golos* (Voice of the people), a Russian newspaper asked the question: "For what Eldora-

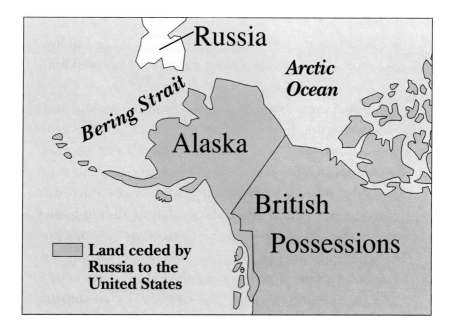

Russia ceded 570,374 square miles to the United States at a cost of about 2¢ an acre.

do does the United States pay us seven million dollars, for the metropolis of Sitka [the center of Alaska's government], consisting of several barbaric country houses and the residence of the colonial governor, and also for several half-century-old windjammers and steamships?"[27]

In mid-May 1867, Alexander signed the treaty and rewarded Stoeckl with $19,000 for his trouble. On June 20, 1867, the two nations formally ratified the treaty.

Seward knew, however, his work had just begun. Though the Senate and the president have the power to ratify treaties, both Houses had to vote on whether to appropriate money to pay for Alaska. Johnson and Seward had many enemies in Congress, as well as those who opposed further expansion of the nation.

Before Congress convened, Brigadier General Lovell H. Rousseau set sail for Sitka. On October 18, 1867, the United States formally took control of Alaska. In a ceremony attended by 250 U.S. troops, the Russian flag was lowered as guns from the *U.S. Ossippee* fired salutes. The Russian flag snagged high up on the 90-foot pole—a strange repeat of the ceremony in New Orleans 64 years before when the U.S. took over that territory from the French. A strong yank ripped the flag's border and wrapped the rest of the cloth firmly around the pole. Finally, a soldier atop a pulley rig pulled the remains of the flag from the pole, and the tattered banner landed on the bayonets below. Embarrassed beyond words, the Russian governor's wife fainted.[28]

The second session of the Fortieth Congress was called to order on December 2, 1867. Thaddeus Stevens, old and ill, made a motion to refer the Alaska matter to the Committee on Foreign Affairs. "When the Constitution, which is the paramount law of the land, declares that we owe a debt," he told his fellow Congressmen, "I should be ashamed to refuse to pay it."[29]

The motion passed, and the question of Alaska's payment passed to the Foreign Affairs Committee. A complication, however, threatened to stall the House vote on the money for Alaska. During the Crimean War, the Russians had made a deal with Benjamin W. Perkins, a Massachusetts sea captain, to provide them with weapons. The war ended before Perkins delivered the guns, but the sea captain maintained that he had lost money on the deal and demanded to be paid. Perkins died in 1860, but his widow continued to push the claim.

Representative Benjamin Butler of Massachusetts and others proposed that $500,000 of the $7.2 million for Alaska go to Perkins's widow to settle her claim. Seward feared such a move would delay payment to Russia and threaten the entire treaty. Representative Nathaniel P. Banks, who headed the Foreign Affairs Committee, had supported the Perkins claim as well. But he assured Seward that he would treat the two matters separately.

In the spring of 1867, Congress was busy with far more urgent matters than Alaska. The battle between President Johnson and Congress had escalated to all-out war. Finally, the Senate voted to impeach—put on trial—Johnson for abusing his powers.

The Committee on Foreign Affairs did not meet until the middle of March to consider the Alaska Purchase. On March 18, the committee postponed further discussion of the matter until May, when the impeachment trial would be over. Under the treaty's terms, the Russians were due to be paid by April 20.

Banks tried to reassure Stoeckl that Congress would approve the Alaskan payment as soon as impeachment proceedings ended. But the Russian minister was furious over the delay. He suggested a tongue-in-cheek solution to his Russian employers: Shame the Americans by offering them Alaska free. Minister Gorchakov quickly vetoed that proposal. He feared the United States, tempted by "American cupidity," would accept.[30]

Instead, Stoeckl hired former senator and newspaperman Robert J. Walker to help the cause. Walker, the irrepressible wordsmith who had lobbied so successfully for the annexation of Texas, was a valuable man to have on the team.

On May 18, as the impeachment trial wound down, the Committee on Foreign Affairs finally met to discuss the Alaska payment. Banks's committee approved it by a small margin. Further action on the matter was postponed once again, this time while the Republicans held their National Convention to nominate a presidential candidate. On May 26, 1867, the Senate voted to acquit President Johnson by one vote, but it was obvious he would never win reelection.

During the delay, Walker pushed the case for Alaska. The former senator from Mississippi favored expansion and had earlier printed articles and passed out pamphlets in favor of the Alaska purchase at Seward's request. Now he stepped up his publicity blitz. He arranged for the *Daily Morning Chronicle*, a Washington, D.C., newspaper owned by D.C. Forney, to print his articles supporting the Alaska purchase. The *National Intelligencer*, another Washington paper, also printed Walker's reports.

It was not until June 30 that Congress began debate on the Alaska purchase. Meeting in the evening because of the heat, proponents and opponents rehashed many of the arguments made earlier in the Senate. Banks focused on Alaska's strategic position, while opponent Cadwallader C. Washburn described the territory as worthless. He also suggested that the House had a Constitutional right to rule on treaties that involved payment.

Frail Thaddeus Stevens, leaning on his cane and

speaking in a shaky voice, rose to refute Washburn's claims. He supported the purchase, he told his colleagues, because, under the Constitution, only the president and the Senate had the right to make treaties. Once the treaty was ratified, he said, the House had no choice but to go along. Stevens, who would die in August, leveled one final barb at those who claimed Alaska was a worthless land of ice. The territory, said Stevens, "is not half so barren as members tried to make out; not half so barren as their brains were in arguing against the bill."[31]

Finally, on July 14, the House approved the payment of $7.2 million to Russia for the Alaskan territory. The vote was 113 to 43, with 44 members abstaining. However, the struggle was not yet ended. As a condition of their approval, House members had added a rider to the bill. The rider claimed that treaties involving payments needed the approval of the House to be ratified.

The Senate, jealously guarding its Constitutional powers, approved the purchase without the rider. Members of both Houses met to work out a compromise. The committee came up with wording that satisfied both houses: that the Alaska treaty "cannot be carried into full force and effect except by legislation to which the consent of both Houses of Congress is necessary."[32]

The House passed its final bill on the matter July 23, 1868, approving the purchase 91 to 48, with 77 abstentions. The Senate agreed to the compromise version of the appropriations bill, and President Johnson signed the Alaska Purchase into law on July 27. Sixteen months had passed since that early morning when Seward and Stoeckl had signed the treaty. The Russian minister shared his disgust with the whole matter in a telegram to Gorchakov informing him of the vote: "I cannot give you an idea of the tribulations and disagreements that I have had to bear before the conclusion of this affair . . . grant me the opportunity to rest for some time in an atmosphere purer than that of Washington."[33]

ALASKA SWINDLE

Stoeckl wasn't the only one who believed Washington had a less than "pure" atmosphere. As soon as the vote was recorded, opponents of the treaty began suggesting that Congressmen had accepted bribes for their favorable votes. The newspapers reported so many rumors about the affair that Congress called a special committee hearing to investigate the charges.

From mid-December until the end of February, the committee heard testimony from newspaper reporters, Walker, U.S. Treasurer Francis Spinner, banker George W. Riggs, and a parade of others. The reporters claimed bribes had been given, but none produced proof to back up their claims.

At the end of the hearing, Congressmen had traced most of the $7.2 million paid by the U.S. Treasury for Alaska. Russia received $7,035,000 of the purchase price. Out of the remaining $165,000 Stoeckl paid Walker $26,000 for his lobbying work, from which Walker paid $5,000 to an associate. Other money, according to Walker's testimony, went to publisher D. W. Forney of the *Chronicle*, who received $3,000 for providing space for Walker's articles. An additional $10,000 was spent by

Stoeckl for telegrams to Russia, and $3,517 went to Riggs as his commission for processing the payment. That left approximately $122,483. Whether Congressmen were bribed or received rewards from Stoeckl was never determined. The committee closed its hearing on the matter without a finding in the case.

Later researchers have found notes in President Johnson's handwriting and in a diary of Seward friend John Bigelow that suggest at least some Congressmen received money in connection with the Alaska Purchase. One writer suggests that the remaining gold went to M.M. Noah, publisher of a California paper favorable to the treaty ($1,000); John Forney, editor of the *Chronicle* ($30,000); and Stoeckl and his Russian assistant Waldemar Bodisco ($21,667). The remaining money (approximately $70,000) was divided among Thaddeus Stevens and ten unknown Congressmen.[34]

Other researchers, however, argue that several on the list, including Stevens, did not have to be bribed because they already supported the treaty. They suggest that Stoeckl and Bodisco may have kept the remaining money for themselves.[35] Regardless of whether the claims were true or false, the Alaska Purchase became associated with scandal.

The Alaska Purchase—Seward's finest achievement—also proved to be the downfall of his expansionist policies. The rumors of wrongdoing tainted attempts to expand the nation's boundaries for many years to come. Proposals to annex Santo Domingo, the Danish Virgin Islands, Samoa, and Hawaii all failed. Thirty years would pass before President McKinley used his political skill in 1898 to

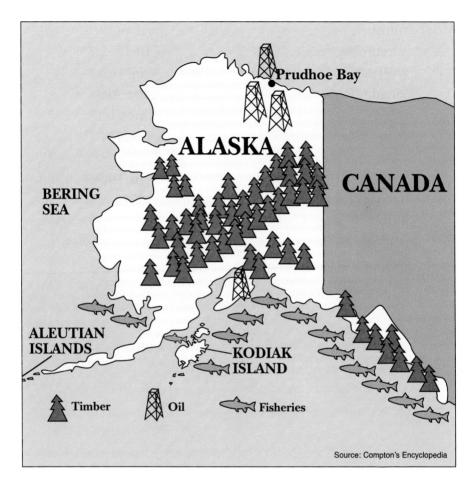

Oil discovered in Alaska's Prudhoe Bay and other resources have brought great wealth to the nation's fiftieth state.

win Congressional approval to annex the islands in the Caribbean and the Pacific.[36]

Nevertheless, the Alaska Purchase was indeed a triumph for Seward. The treaty added 570,374 square miles to the nation's territory, at a cost of about 2¢ an acre. Far from being a frozen wasteland, Alaska has proved to be extremely valuable to the United States. In 1898, the discovery of gold in the neighboring Yukon Territory of Canada brought thousands of settlers to the Alaskan territory. Its coal, salmon fisheries, copper mines, oil, timber, and other resources have produced billions of dollars' worth of products for the nation.[37]

Oil was discovered in Prudhoe Bay in 1968. Since then oil companies have paid more than $900 million to dig and operate Alaskan oil wells.[38] On July 28, 1977, Alaska's "black gold" was pumped through the territory's first pipeline. That one oil shipment was valued at $7.2 million, the price Americans paid for "Seward's Folly."[39]

Source Notes

INTRODUCTION

1. Russell, Francis, *The American Heritage History of the Making of the Nation* (New York: American Heritage Publishing Co., 1968), pp. 74–75.
2. *Portland Gazette* (July 4, 1803), p. 1.
3. Clinton, Susan, *Cornerstones of Freedom: The Story of Seward's Folly* (Chicago: Childrens Press, 1987), p. 16.

CHAPTER ONE

1. Adams, Henry, *History of the United States of America During the Administrations of Thomas Jefferson* (New York: The Library of America, 1986), p. 241.
2. Ibid.
3. Ibid., p. 265.
4. Ibid., p. 280.
5. Dangerfield, George, *Chancellor Robert R. Livingston of New York, 1746–1813* (New York: Harcourt, Brace and Co., 1960), p. 323.
6. Ibid., p. 330.
7. Ibid., p. 337.
8. Ibid.
9. Adams, p. 300.
10. Morgan, George, *The Life of James Monroe* (Boston: Small, Maynard and Co., 1921), p. 240.
11. Dangerfield, p. 366.
12. Adams, p. 315.

13. Dangerfield, p. 362.
14. Phelan, Mary Kay, *The Story of the Louisiana Purchase* (New York: Thomas Y. Crowell, 1979), pp. 81–83. The passages quoted in 14–16 are originally from Lucien Bonaparte's memoirs.
15. Adams, p. 326.
16. Ibid.
17. Ibid., p. 319.
18. Gilman, Daniel C., *James Monroe* (New York: Houghton, Mifflin and Co., 1899), p. 86.
19. Adams, p. 324.
20. Ibid.
21. Dangerfield, p. 366.
22. Ibid.
23. Ibid., p. 250.
24. Adams, p. 347.
25. Adams, pp. 357–358.
26. *Portland Gazette* (July 4, 1803), p. 1.
27. Morgan, p. 252.
28. Adams, p. 363.
29. Ibid., p. 373.
30. Ibid., pp. 340–341.
31. *Portland Gazette* (May 16, 1803), p. 1.
32. *Portland Gazette* (May 23, 1803), p. 1.
33. Morgan, p. 253.
34. Ibid.
35. Ibid.
36. Adams, pp. 334–335.

OTHER REFERENCES

Dufour, Charles L., *Ten Flags in the Wind: The Story of*

Louisiana (New York: Harper & Row, 1967).

Winwar, Frances, *Napoleon and the Battle of Waterloo* (New York: Random House, 1953).

Gayarré, William, *History of Louisiana: The Spanish Dominations* (New York: William J. Widdleton, 1867).

CHAPTER TWO

1. Paxson, Frederic L. Paxson, *History of the American Frontier, 1763–1893* (Cambridge, Mass.: Houghton Mifflin Co., 1924), p. 184.
2. Gilman, p. 374.
3. Russell, p. 231.
4. Paxson, p. 307.
5. Ibid., pp. 306–307.
6. Long, Jeffery, *Duel of Eagles: The Mexican and U.S. Fight for the Alamo* (New York: William Morrow and Co., 1990), p. 59.
7. Ibid., p. 60.
8. Ibid.
9. Ibid., p. 119.
10. Ibid., p. 121.
11. Ibid., p. 212.
12. Ibid., p. 230.
13. Ibid., p. 232.
14. Ibid., p. 253.
15. Ibid., p. 259.
16. Ibid., pp. 284–285.
17. Ibid., pp. 312–313.
18. Ibid., p. 313.
19. Ibid., p. 316.
20. Merk, Frederick, *Fruits of Propaganda in the Tyler Ad-*

ministration (Cambridge, Mass.: Harvard University Press, 1971), p. 96.

21. Russell, p. 240.

22. Merk, p. 98.

23. Ibid., p. 100.

24. Ibid.

25. Ibid., pp. 101–102.

26. Ibid., p. 124.

27. Seitz, Don C., *The "Also Rans": Great Men Who Missed Making the Presidential Goal* (New York: Thomas Y. Crowell Co., 1928), p. 88.

28. Russell, p. 258.

29. Van Alstyne, R.W., *The Rising American Empire* (New York: Oxford University Press, 1960), p. 141.

30. Russell, p. 260.

31. Seitz, p. 96.

32. Price, Glenn W., *Origins of the War with Mexcio: The Polk-Stockton Intrigue* (Austin, Texas: University of Texas Press, 1967), p. 158.

33. Russell, p. 263.

34. Ibid., p. 265.

35. Ibid.

36. Billington, Ray Allen, *Westward Expansion: A History of the American Frontier* (New York: Macmillan Co., 1960), p. 584.

37. Russell, p. 272.

38. Ibid., p. 274.

39. Billington, p. 574.

OTHER REFERENCES

Kolodny, Annette, *The Land Before Her: Fantasy and Expe-*

rience of the American Frontiers, 1630–1860 (Chapel Hill, N.C.: University of North Carolina Press, 1984).

CHAPTER THREE

1. Farrar, Victor J.,*The Annexation of Russian America to the United States* (New York: Russell & Russell, 1966), pp. 112–113.
2. Jensen, Ronald J., *The Alaska Purchase and Russian-American Relations* (Seattle: University of Washington Press, 1975), p. 63.
3. Gibson, James R., *Imperial Russia inFrontier America* (New York: Oxford University Press, 1976), p. 8.
4. Higginson, Ella, *Alaska the Great Country* (New York: Macmillan Co., 1909), pp. 165–166.
5. Ibid., p. 178.
6. Jensen, p. 9.
7. Ibid., p. 5.
8. Ibid., p. 8.
9. Ibid.
10. Ibid., p. 10.
11. Ibid., p. 16.
12. Ibid., p. 36.
13. Ibid., p. 49.
14. Ibid., p. 27.
15. Clinton, p. 10.
16. Jensen, p. 44.
17. Ibid., p. 62.
18. Ibid., p. 75.
19. Ibid.
20. Ibid., pp. 75–76.
21. Ibid., p. 76.

22. Ibid., p. 100.

23. Clinton, p. 18.

24. Jensen, p. 84.

25. Ibid., p. 85.

26. Ibid., pp. 89–90.

27. Ibid., pp. 96–97.

28. Ibid., p. 101.

29. Ibid., p. 104.

30. Ibid., p. 109.

31. Ibid., p. 116.

32. Farrar, p. 93.

33. Jensen, pp. 120–121.

34. Ibid., p. 130.

35. Holbo, Paul S., *Tarnished Expansion: The Alaska Scandal, the Press, and Congress, 1867–1871* (Knoxville, Tenn.: The University of Tennessee Press, 1983), p. 50.

36. Ibid., p. 97.

37. *Information Please Almanac 1995*, 48th Edition (New York: Houghton Mifflin Co., 1995), p. 750.

38. Clinton, p. 29.

39. Heinrichs, Ann, *America the Beautiful: Alaska* (Chicago: Childrens Press, 1991), p. 59.

OTHER REFERENCES

Seitz, Don C., *The "Also Rans": Great Men Who Missed Making the Presidential Goal* (New York: Thomas Y. Crowell Co., 1928).

FURTHER READING

Bill, Alfred Hoyt. *Rehearsal for Conflict: The War with Mexico, 1846–1848*. New York: History Book Club, 1947.

Callcott, Wilfrid Hardy. *Santa Anna: The Story of an Enigma Who Once Was Mexico*. Hamden, Conn.: Archon Books, 1964.

Carroll, Bob. *Napoleon Bonaparte*. San Diego: Lucent Books, 1994.

Chidsey, Donald. *Louisiana Purchase*. New York: Crown, 1972.

Clinton, Susan. *Cornerstones of Freedom: The Story of Seward's Folly*. Chicago: Childrens Press, 1987.

Davis, Burke. *Old Hickory: A Life of Andrew Jackson*. New York: Dial Press, 1977.

Dufour, Charles L. *Ten Flags in the Wind: The Story of Louisiana*. New York: Harper & Row, 1967.

Fehrenbach, T. R. *Lone Star: A History of Texas and Texans*. New York: American Legacy Press, 1983.

Fisher, Leonard Everett. *The Alamo*. New York: Holiday House, 1987.

Friend, Llerena. *Sam Houston: The Great Designer*. Austin: University of Texas Press, 1954.

Glover, Michael. *The Napoleonic Wars: An Illustrated History: 1792–1815*. New York: Hippocrene Books, 1978.

Haley, James L. *Texas: An Album of History*. Garden City, N.Y.: Doubleday & Company, 1985.

Heinrichs, Ann. *America the Beautiful: Alaska*. Chicago: Childrens Press, 1991.

Henry, Robert Selph. *The Story of the Mexican War*. New York: Bobbs-Merrill Co., 1950.

Huston, Cleburne. *Deaf Smith: Incredible Texas Spy*. Waco: Texian Press, 1973.

Kolodny, Annette. *The Land Before Her: Fantasy and Experience of the American Frontiers, 1630–1860*. Chapel Hill, N.C.: The University of North Carolina Press, 1984

Lee, Rebecca Smith. *Mary Austin Holley: A Biography*. Austin: University of Texas Press, 1962.

Lofaro, Michael A. *Davy Crockett: The Man, The Legend, The Legacy, 1786–1986*. Knoxville: University of Tennessee Press, 1985.

Long, Jeffery. *Duel of Eagles: The Mexican and U.S. Fight for the Alamo*. New York: William Morrow and Co., 1990.

Nardo, Don. *The Mexican-American War*. San Diego: Lucent Books, 1991.

Phelan, Mary Kay. *The Story of the Louisiana Purchase*. New York: Thomas Y. Crowell, 1979.

Riding, Alan. *Distant Neighbors: A Portrait of the Mexicans*. New York: Alfred A. Knopf, 1985.

Russell, Francis. *The American Heritage History of the Making of the Nation*. New York: American Heritage Publishing Co., 1968.

Smith, Page. *Daughters of the Promised Land: Women in American History*. Boston: Little, Brown, 1979.

Tallant, Robert. *The Louisiana Purchase*. New York: Random House, 1952.

Tinkle, Lon. *13 Days to Glory*. College Station: Texas A&M University Press, 1985.

INDEX